POWERHOUSE:
100 YEARS OF KEMET ELECTRONICS

Bradford Verter

The Winthrop Group, Inc.

POWERHOUSE: 100 YEARS OF KEMET ELECTRONICS

Copyright © 2020 KEMET ELECTRONICS CORPORATION
Produced by THE WINTHROP GROUP, INC.
All rights reserved.
Printed in USA.

The Library of Congress has catalogued this publication as follows:
The Winthrop Group, POWERHOUSE: 100 YEARS OF KEMET ELECTRONICS
ISBN 978-0-578-63874-4

For additional information about KEMET ELECTRONICS CORPORATION visit **www.kemet.com**.

Today, we are proud to celebrate KEMET's centennial as a visionary, worldwide organization dedicated to making the world a better, safer, more connected place to live. But the scale of our achievement didn't happen overnight. In 1919, the people who founded KEMET never expected their modest enterprise in Cleveland, Ohio to one day span the globe. Nor did they envision the many technological advances that KEMET has made possible: communication satellites, cellphones, supersonic jets, space stations, personal computers, and electric cars — innovations that touch every household, helping improve our lives.

In very real ways, the story of how we got here is the story of the creation of the modern world. It is a story about technology and dedicated people, whose ingenuity and perseverance shaped our success. At KEMET, we believe that our employees at every level, and in every location, are our most valuable assets. These are the people who built KEMET over the past 100 years, and who will continue to drive us to new possibilities in the century to come.

Please join me in honoring their achievements. This is their story, our story — the story of KEMET.

William M. Lowe, Jr.
Chief Executive Officer

CONTENTS

A CENTURY OF INNOVATION

Fᴿᴏᴍ ɪᴛꜱ ʜᴜᴍʙʟᴇ ᴏʀɪɢɪɴꜱ ɪɴ ᴛʜᴇ ꜱɪᴍᴘʟᴇ ᴡᴏʀᴋꜱʜᴏᴘ ᴏꜰ ᴀ ʏᴏᴜɴɢ, entrepreneurial inventor to its rise as a global leader in the electronics industry, KEMET has been and remains a powerhouse. Like the small electrical components the company has long produced, KEMET is the quiet, unrecognized force behind so many of the technological advances that have shaped the modern world. KEMET products helped radios reach millions of homes during the Great Depression. They helped the Allies win World War II. They helped put a man on the moon. They made cars safer and airplanes more secure. They fueled the development of television, computers, mobile phones, and the Internet. Today KEMET is designing new materials to further the revolution in green energy, electric vehicles, communications, artificial intelligence and the Internet of Things (IoT). Although KEMET is not a household name, its products are in every household, and will be long into the future.

KEMET's growth does not represent a linear path, nor was its success inevitable. Many of the companies that started at the same time as KEMET, including much larger firms, failed along the way. The failure of other companies is no discredit to them — the electronics industry is famously volatile, with technologies and markets shifting so fast that many companies have collapsed trying to keep up. The fact that KEMET not only survived, but thrived, is testament to the quality of its work and the foresight of its people.

In the century spanning from 1919 to 2019, the electronics industry was born, rebuilt, and transfigured multiple times. Sometimes this was counterintuitive —

based on the dictates of purchasers and consumers, wartime demands, national rivalries, relentless globalization, and continuous invention. In 1919, who could have predicted the prevalence of television? In 1950, who could have predicted the dominance of the Internet? KEMET stayed relevant through so many technological revolutions not only because of its products, but because of its people.

KEMET's birth was due to the entrepreneurship of one man, Hugh Spencer Cooper, who — like Alexander Graham Bell, Guglielmo Marconi, and Thomas Alva Edison before him — was a largely self-taught inventor. He churned out one brilliant idea after another, but continuously divided his energies by pursuing multiple unrelated projects simultaneously. KEMET's growth was due to a giant corporation, Union Carbide and Carbon, which took Cooper's inventions and channeled them to productive use. It was the directors of Union Carbide who redefined KEMET from being a freewheeling idea factory into one of the mainstays of the electronics industry. This was realized first through the production of getters (a device that allows vacuum tubes to operate efficiently), then through the production of capacitors (a device that helps regulate the flow and storage of energy in an electronic apparatus, from hearing aids to space stations). KEMET's success was due to the decision of its managers to form an independent company after the breakup of Union Carbide, and to take well considered risks that paid off handsomely.

This is the story of how KEMET became the hidden force responsible for the technological wonders that defined our past and that will continue to define our future. It is the story of the people who built a powerhouse.

CHAPTER ONE:
UNALLOYED INVENTION

KEMET WAS FOUNDED BEFORE THERE WAS SUCH A THING AS AN 'ELECTRONICS industry,' back when radio was new, space travel was the stuff of fantasy, and the Internet would have seemed a madman's dream. In the first decades of the twentieth century, mechanical inventions, electricity, and chemical engineering were all emergent, but still highly experimental fields, pioneered by an enterprising generation of inventors and entrepreneurs. The man who created the company that would become KEMET was Hugh Spencer Cooper (1885-1971). He was born on Christmas Eve, in Cleveland, Ohio, a land of technological marvels. Just six years earlier, local inventor Charles Brush had flipped the switch that illuminated the city with his invention, a carbon arc lamp. People traveled hundred of miles to Cleveland to see the new system of street lighting — brighter, more efficient and less costly than the gaslights that had defined the Victorian era. Like many Clevelanders of his generation, Cooper was determined to follow in Brush's footsteps. For the rest of his life he would be an enthusiastic experimenter and inventor.

Hugh Spencer Cooper (1885-1971), Founder of KEMET.

However, Cooper's first passion was not electronics, but metals. This was not surprising, given his upbringing. Cooper's father, John Cooper (1847-1930), was the son of British immigrants and worked as a 'puddler' in a local iron mill. Just like it sounds, the work of a puddler was to melt pig iron in a reverberatory furnace and carefully stir, until it hit the right consistency. At this point, the scorching metal would be allowed to run out into a puddle, before it was collected. Working long, strenuous hours in a sweaty iron factory was dangerous, hellish work that required constant attention. A small mistake could result in delays, ruined product, or even catastrophic burns and other injuries. It was a grueling life — all designed to make processed iron less brittle than iron simply melted. By 1900, John Cooper had aged out of puddling and was working as an engineer at an industrial bakery, but the metallurgy of these early years undoubtedly shaped how young Hugh Cooper thought of the world. Hugh almost certainly worked as an apprentice with his father, and although it was his father's profession, he would soon make a version of it his own.[1]

1885
Birth of
Hugh S. Cooper.

1915
Cooper obtains
first patent for
a new alloy.

1917
Cooper and
associates found
Cooper Research
Company
and General Alloys.

Union Carbide
and Carbon
Corporation (UCC)
organized through
the merger of five
companies.

1919
Cooper sells patents
to Union Carbide,
establishes KEMET
Laboratories as a
R&D division,
focusing on alloys
of rare metals.

1924
KEMET develops
barium getter.

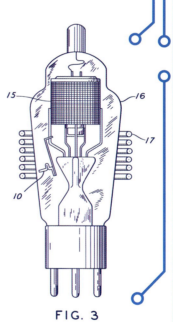

15   16

17

10

FIG. 3

1933
KEMET shifts
its primary focus
from R&D to
manufacturing.
Its getters will
soon be featured
in virtually every
vacuum tube
manufactured in
the United States
and England.

1939-1946
KEMET's
workforce
triples as the
company
produces
getters for
vacuum tubes
needed during
WWII.

1947-1954
KEMET's workforce
doubles again to
meet the demand
for getters for
cathode tubes
used in a rapidly
growing television
market.

Margaret A. Hittle, Steel Mill. *1909*

Hugh Cooper's route was not a direct one, however. A young man had to learn a trade, and in 1904 he enrolled at the Cleveland School of Pharmacy, part of a network of schools that would later amalgamate to form Case Western University. At the turn of the century, many fields that would become established, professional disciplines in the coming decades were not yet fully formed. One could learn chemistry, the branch of science dealing with the fundamental building blocks of nature, through attending university. But pharmaceutical studies gave one the same basic education. The druggists of these days worked with suppliers to secure compounds that could be mixed to create substances according to widely circulated recipes, as well as idiosyncratic, proprietary concoctions of their own design. Drugstores also sold other household goods that relied on the practical use of chemistry. Many druggists applied their training in chemistry to a wide range of purpose. In addition to drugs, one Cleveland pharmacy, Palmer and Sackrider, also sold their own medical supplies alongside window glass, house paints, distilled whiskies, and locally made wines.

In 1907, at the age of 21, Hugh Cooper passed the state exam to receive his pharmacy certification, and in the coming years he opened a local drug store in Cleveland.[2] At the time, the neighborhood of Cleveland in which Hugh was operating was a dynamic, commercial hub, and competition was fierce. A generation earlier, in the late 1870s, there were already more than 30 pharmacies in the area, including several that would later develop into drugstore chains. Market saturation meant that pharmacists, like Cooper, had to specialize. Some offered cut-rate prices; others catered to an exclusive clientele or focused on unique, proprietary products. In this environment, pharmacists were entrepreneurs who either distinguished themselves or quickly folded.[3] That Hugh Cooper's drugstore was still in business in the mid 1910s, several years after opening, was a testament to his ability.

But Cooper was not content to operate as a pharmacist indefinitely, and he used his professional credentials to acquire a range of other, experimental materials — chemical substances that would been unavailable to others. Given his father's work and his own experience in an iron mill, Cooper gravitated toward metallurgy, specifically related to the functioning of electrical contact

continued on page 10

A restaurant (lower left corner) occupies the site in Cleveland where Cooper operated a pharmacy before he founded KEMET. His drugstore would have occupied the front of the shop, his experimental lab in the back.

INDUSTRIAL CLEVELAND

By 1919, Cleveland was one of the nation's leading hubs for industrial production, technological innovation, and economic entrepreneurship. Rapid population growth was one reason for this. The city hit its peak in the period 1910-1940, with a population of between 3 and 3.5 million, making it the fifth largest in the nation. The rich ore resources of Northeast Ohio gave birth to a thriving metal working industry, making Cleveland second only to Chicago and equal to Pittsburgh as a center for mining and manufacturing. Clevelanders originally took advantage of the Great Lakes system and the Ohio River to transport their goods; later, railroads carried the fruits of the city across the growing nation. Rapid industrial growth gave rise to a new class of wealthy entrepreneurs eager to invest in new enterprises. In the Great Lakes region only Chicago had more millionaires than Cleveland.

Abundant natural resources and capital combined to make Cleveland a center not only for manufacture but also for innovation. The region

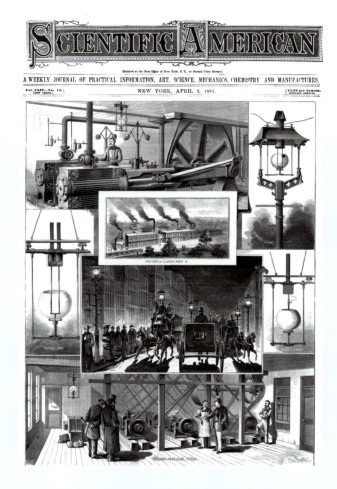

A 1881 issue of Scientific American *celebrated the ways the carbon arc lamps developed in Cleveland were transforming the urban landscape.*

spawned inventors like Hugh S. Cooper who drew on a rich base of expertise in metal working developed over generations. The Case Institute of Technology (later incorporated into Case Western University), founded in 1880, provided a training ground for young scientists. In 1900, Cleveland ranked eighth in the nation in terms of the number of patents, almost all of which derived from local industrial production.

Charles F. Brush examines an arc lamp in the basement of his house in Cleveland, 1929.

Cleveland's most important inventor was Charles F. Brush, who was the first to patent a dynamo to generate electricity and the first to develop a system of lighting that made Cleveland the first city in the world with electric street lamps. Brush hired the best, and his employees went on to found major enterprises that grew from the products of his inventions. These included companies devoted to electric light and power, electrical machinery, steel, petroleum, chemical, automobiles — all centerpieces of what was widely recognized as a Second Industrial Revolution. It was one of Brush's supervisors, W. H. Bolton, who recognized that the spread of arc lighting would create a demand for carbon electrodes, and founded the company that would become National Carbon, which would in the 1930s be home to KEMET. **K**

points in machinery, such as automcbiles. As he explained it, "at that time, platinum contact points were universally used in magnetos and I undertook to find a cheaper material." It was a savvy, careful decision. Focusing on the properties and industrial applications of rare metals would not require the type of sophisticated, expensive equipment required for more traditional, well known experimentation. It also required a comparatively small financial outlay, and the field was wide open. Any success had the potential to be capitalized upon quickly.

UNITED STATES PATENT OFFICE.

HUGH S. COOPER, OF CLEVELAND, OHIO, ASSIGNOR TO THE ELECTRO METALS PRODUCTS COMPANY, OF CLEVELAND, OHIO.

METAL ALLOY.

1,229,037.   Specification of Letters Patent.   **Patented June 5, 1917.**

No Drawing.   Application filed August 14, 1915. Serial No. 45,526.

To all whom it may concern:

Be it known that I, HUGH S. COOPER, a citizen of the United States, residing at Cleveland, in the county of Cuyahoga and State of Ohio, have invented certain new and useful Improvements in Metal Alloys, of which the following is a specification.

My invention appertains to a metal alloy adapted to be used as a substitute for platinum in the electrical art, as in coils, magnetos and all vibrating instruments, and the invention consists of a composition of silver and other metals which is ductile, and malleable, and of comparatively high melting point, good electrical conductivity, great hardness, non-oxidizing, and producible at a low cost.

In all compositions of alloys known to me in which silver enters, copper is also used but I find that this composition oxidizes very readily making it useless for electrical contact purposes, especially where the contact is exposed to high temperatures and severe usage. I also find that it is not practicable to use silver alone as it is too soft and the melting point is not high enough. However, silver is a good electrical conductor and relatively cheap as compared with platinum and when alloyed in proper proportions with other metals as hereinafter described serves as an excellent substitute for platinum. One such composition comprises silver, palladium and cobalt, in substantially the following proportions: seventy per cent. of silver, twenty-five per cent. of palladium, and five per cent. of cobalt. Platinum may be substituted for the palladium with equally good results, and nickel for the cobalt, but I prefer palladium as it may be obtained at a lower cost than platinum. I also prefer cobalt as I find it resists oxidization at a higher temperature than nickel, and it also makes a harder alloy. In this alloy I use as little of platinum or palladium as possible consistent with the durability and lasting qualities of the product, and I also find that three to five per cent. of cobalt or nickel is sufficient to furnish the hardness necessary.

What I claim is:

1. An alloy for electrical uses, comprising silver and one or more of the metals of the platinum group and a metal of the cobalt-nickel group in substantially the proportions stated.

2. An alloy for electrical uses containing silver, palladium, and a metal of the cobalt-nickel group in the proportions substantially set forth.

3. An alloy for electrical contact purposes composed of silver, palladium, and cobalt in approximately the proportions stated as to make the alloy hard, heat resisting, non-oxidizing and a good electrical conductor.

4. A metal alloy composed of seventy per cent. of silver, twenty-five per cent. of palladium, and five per cent. cobalt.

In testimony whereof I affix my signature in presence of two witnesses.

HUGH S. COOPER.

Witnesses:
J. W. FRASER,
R. B. MOSER.

Cuyahoga Building, Cleveland. The administrative offices of Cooper Company before 1919.

By 1915, he had his first major breakthrough. That year, Cooper developed two new alloys: the first, of silver, palladium, and cobalt; and the second, of gold, silver, and osmium. The alloys could serve as electrical conductors, and Cooper patented them under the name of the Electro Metals Products Company. Perhaps unsurprisingly, he soon found buyers. "I sold about $40,000.00 worth of these contacts to the K.W. Ignition Company of Cleveland," Cooper wrote. This was a very lucrative enterprise — $40,000 in 1917 is the equivalent of about $780,000 in 2019 dollars. But the market for these products was also short lived, as the rapid pace of invention soon led to new technologies that replaced magneto systems with battery ignition systems in automobiles.[4]

Opposite: The first patent filed by the brilliant young inventor who would found KEMET. He was a few months shy of his 30th birthday at the time.

Although the success of his initial discovery was cut short, Cooper's early achievement opened the door for more expansive experimentation, particularly with rare metals, at a time when the field was wide open. Just a few years later, for example, one of Cooper's colleagues would decry how scientists and industrialist ignored metals that were perceived to be useless, overlooking their potential:

 When an element is condemned as being useless, it is evident that its characteristic properties are deeply hidden. We who are interested in the commercial application of the rare metals, ought to be thankful that we are working at this period, for these substances are being launched upon their journey through the commercial world as never before. It is our duty to assist in this project.[5]

Following his initial discoveries related to magneto alloys, Cooper forged a partnership with George P. Koelliker, an officer at the Citizens Savings and Trust Company, to organize capital investment to support future research and new ventures. In October 1916, they founded the Cooper Company with three other investors, to develop and manufacture alloys, with a capital stock of $30,000 (the equivalent of about $700,000 in 2019). In 1917, another, separate company was formed, Cooper Research, with a capital stock of $15,000, which was tasked with developing chemical and metallurgical products. The Cooper Company opened its office in the Cuyahoga Building; Cooper Research established a laboratory in Cleveland, Ohio, at 4503 Euclid Avenue.

Work in Cooper's research lab took off. In 1917-1918, Cooper secured a series of patents for a new alloy of zirconium (the first alloy to use it) and nickel that he dubbed, "Cooperite." As Cooper explained, his new alloy offered a superior alternative to Stellite, a chromium alloy resistant to corrosion that had been around for a decade.

With the discovery, Cooper and Koelliker created a third company, General Alloys, to market Cooperite, organizing tests n Sheffield, England, to demonstrate that the alloy could be used in tool manufacturing. The move, however, never paid off. In part, as a result of the changing economy during the First World War, the company eventually went bankrupt.[7] But it was by no means Cooper's only focus.

In adcition to inventing Cooperite, Cooper developed a deep fascination with beryllium. Most commonly found in beryl, the metal had been discovered in 1798 by the French chemist Louis Nicolas Vauquelin, but it proved difficult to isolate in a pure form. And its pure form held significant potential, including in alloys associated with electrical components and, eventually, high tech structural materials. Experiments in France (1898) and Germany (1913) had produced a few grains of purified beryllium, but no one had yet learned how to isolate more of it — until Cooper. In 1916, he developed a process to produce the first sizeable ingot of metal beryllium. The following year, he patented the discovery, and in the decades ahead, the study and development of beryllium would continue to capture Cooper's interest, at KEMET and elsewhere.[8]

> **"** *Cooperite is the newest and best alloy known for use in the manufacture of edge tools of all descriptions, mainly machine tools for milling cutters, cast tools for lathe and plane use, etc. Owing to the fact that the alloy remains in liquid state for a considerable period before solidifying it is possible to make castings with great ease; and so far as known is the first alloy discovered from which intricate machine tools can be made successfully.[6]* **"**

4503-05 Euclid Ave.

S 194 6-12-45

KEMET Laboratories was located on the second floor at 4503 Euclid Avenue from 1919 to 1933.

The breakthroughs with beryllium, combined with the potential of Cooperite, were also significant enough to catch the attention of the directors of the Union Carbide and Carbon Corporation (Union Carbide), the research and manufacturing conglomerate. In 1919, Union Carbide struck a deal with Cooper and his partners. In exchange for dissolving their companies and transferring their patents to Union Carbide, Cooper and his partners would receive 10,000 shares of Union Carbide stock (then valued at $750,000 — or almost $11 million in 2019 dollars — no small sum). Cooper would continue on as research director of a new company that would be located at the current Cooper Research Company facilities. Officers of Union Carbide would take a majority share in the new company, with Koelliker and Cooper holding the rest. The acquisition of Cooper's outfit brought him into a dynamic, complex conglomerate and created KEMET Laboratories, its name drawn from Cooper's own passion: CHEMical-METallurgical.[9]

Cooper's new alloy, introduced as a superior alternative to Stellite, attracted the notice of Union Carbide.

Cutting Tools Which Contain No Iron

Some more data are now given out regarding the non-ferrous cutting tool for cutting steel known as Cooperite. It is a departure for the leading material for cutting tools, both plain or high speed, in steel. This new material has nickel as its basis, the other components being tungsten, silicon, molybdenum and aluminum with a proportion up to 15 percent of zirconium. During the war it was made in this country on a semicommercial scale and used for turning shells and a plant for it production and the manufacture of tools of all kinds is being erected at Kokomo, Ind.

Turning tools made of Cooperite are cast and then ground to shape, without any forging or heat treatment. They are described as being tough, with a fine silky fracture and free from shrinkage and blowholes and it is stated that they can be used for the bulk of engineering operations except those for which specially thin tools are required. In tests made by the Sheffield Testing Company the alloy was put in competition on lathe roughing, with the standard high speed steel used by that company, which is declared to be superior to the majority of Sheffield high speed steels. In one series of tests, in which the tools were ¾ inch square, the depth of cut 3/16 inch, the traverse per revolution 1/16 inch and the cutting speed 123 feet a minute, the weight of material removed from the test bar was 4.85 pounds per minute. The tool of standard high speed steel was reported "done up" after 2¾ minutes' work, while one piece of Cooperite lasted 14 minutes 39 seconds and was then "slightly worn but still cutting," and another, rather harder, worked 9 minutes 6 seconds before it was done up. A demonstration of the melting of the material and the casting of tools was given at the works of the Sheffield Mercantile Steel Company, and the tools made were then tested by the testing company undr conditions similar to those already described, except that the cutting speed was 120 feet a minute. A Cooperite tool lasted 21 minutes 20 seconds, while one of the best high speed steel broke down after 2 minutes 20 seconds.

KEMET LABORATORIES COMPANY, INC.

Annual Meeting of Common Stockholders, January 12, 1920

CERTIFICATE OF INSPECTORS OF ELECTION

We, the undersigned duly appointed inspectors of election of KEMET LABORATORIES COMPANY, INC., a stock corporation, do hereby certify as follows:

That the annual meeting of stockholders of said corporation was held at the office of said corporation in the City of Niagara Falls, New York, on the 12th day of January, A. D. 1920, at 12 o'clock noon, pursuant to a waiver of notice and the By-Laws of said corporation.

That before entering upon the discharge of our duties we were severally sworn to faithfully execute the duties of inspectors at said meeting with strict impartiality and according to the best of our ability, and the oath so taken has been subscribed by us and is hereto annexed.

That the result of the vote taken at said meeting for the election of directors of said corporation for the ensuing year and until their successors shall be elected and qualified, was as follows:

W. J. Knapp	2000 shares
G. H. Reid	2000 shares
G. P. Koelliker	2000 shares
G. C. Furness	2000 shares
Hugh S. Cooper	2000 shares

That said W. J. Knapp, G. H. Reid, G. P. Koelliker, G.C. Furness, and Hugh S. Cooper, having received a plurality of the votes cast, were declared by us duly elected directors of said corporation for the ensuing year and until their successors shall be elected and qualified.

IN WITNESS WHEREOF, we have made and signed this certificate the 12th day of January, A. D. 1920.

James H Critchett

Charles O. Jacoby

STATE OF NEW YORK) ss:
COUNTY OF NIAGARA)

On this 12th day of January, A. D. 1920, before me personally came C. O. Jacoby and J. H. Critchett, to me known and known to me to be the individuals described in and who executed the foregoing certificate and severally acknowledged to me that they executed the same.

Henry B. Hageman
Notary Public

KEMET's first board of directors included Cooper and his early business partner, George Koelliker. Representatives of Union Carbide included William J. Knapp, son of Union Carbide's president, and George Furness, who would soon change the course of research at KEMET.

In 1917, the five interconnected and interdependent companies that had been offshoots of enterprises founded by Morehead and Brush combined to become United Carbide and Carbon (Union Carbide). It was a move that gave the company greater economies of scale, also allowing the consolidated company to explore research and development in directions that would never have been feasible for any individual, smaller firm. The framework was critical to the early

continued on page 18

UNION CARBIDE AND CARBON CORPORATION

Union Carbide, creator of KEMET Laboratories, had itself been recently formed through the union of five companies:

The Union Carbide Company

After the Civil War, James Turner Morehead (1840-1908), was determined to rebuild the South through diverse economic development. He owned cotton mills in Spray (now Eden), NC, which ran by water power. Seeking new uses for the excess energy, he hired a young Canadian inventor, Thomas L. Willson (1860-1915), who had invented an electric arc furnace capable of smelting ore. Taking advantage of rich local mineral deposits, the two established the Willson Aluminum Company in 1890. (The company never actually made aluminum). An accidental discovery produced in one of Willson's furnaces yielded a new compound, calcium carbide. Calcium carbide was unique because it could produce a highly flammable gas called acetylene when mixed with water. Acetylene created brighter light and more heat than was otherwise available, and Morehead quickly capitalized on the industrial possibilities, forming the Electro Gas Company to sell franchises to manufacture calcium carbide. Among the licensees was George O. Knapp (1855-1945) of the Peoples Gas Light and Coke Company of Chicago. In 1898, Knapp and the tycoon Cornelius

Kingsley Garrison Billings (1861-1937) joined with Morehead and his son, John Motley Morehead III (1870-1965) — a chemist who had apprenticed with Willson — to found Union Carbide.[1]

The National Carbon Company

Washington H. Lawrence (1840-1900) had worked under Charles F. Brush to produce the arc lamps that electrified Cleveland, New York, and other cities. Brush's lights depended upon a ready supply of carbon electrodes, so in 1886, Lawrence established a partnership with several other executives, including the son of President Rutherford B. Hayes, to form the National Carbon Company. In 1896, the company marketed the first battery intended for home use. National Carbon produced a wide variety of carbon materials, but their signature product would always be Eveready batteries.

Prest-O-Lite

In 1904, entrepreneur Percy C. Avery approached Carl Fisher (1874-1939) and James Allison (1872-1928), partners in an Indianapolis automotive firm, with the idea of equipping cars with headlights fueled by acetylene compressed into portable containers. Electric lights on automobiles had not yet been invented, and mounted lanterns were the norm. Together they formed the Concentrated Acetylene Company, which in 1906 was changed to Prest-O-Lite, the name of their signature product. (Later, Fisher and Allison would also found the

Indianapolis Motor Speedway.) Acetylene linked the company with Union Carbide, and Prest-O-Lite car batteries linked the company to National Carbon.[2]

The Linde Air Products Company

Carl von Linde (1842-1934), a German scientist focusing on refrigeration systems, developed a process for liquifying oxygen and other components of air in 1895, but encountered difficulty registering his patent in the United States because of an earlier patent on air liquification. Charles Brush learned of the dispute and offered to fight on Linde's behalf in return for an interest in his patents. They won in 1903, and in 1907 Brush and von Linde established the Linde Air Products Company, headquartered in Cleveland and Buffalo, NY. The hydrogen, oxygen, and other gases produced by Linde would become crucial components for a newly emerging chemical industry.[3]

The Electro-Metallurgical Company

In 1896, the Willson Aluminum plant in Spray, NC, burned down. Rather than rebuild it, James T. Morehead established a new experimental station in Holcomb Rock, VA, and another in Glen Ferris, WV. These plants produced ferroalloys, which could be used for projectiles and armor plating to supply the U.S. military during the Spanish-American War. Edgar F. Price (1873-1935), who had worked at Spray, moved to Niagara Falls, NY, to oversee operations at a calcium carbide plant, recently acquired by Union Carbide. Price reorganized Willson Aluminum and acquired an independent research facility headed by the brilliant materials scientist Frederick Mark Becket. The Electro-Metallurgical Company (Electromet), incorporated in West Virginia in 1906, would focus on developing ferro-metal alloys, tungsten, titanium, and later, uranium.[4]

Linked by overlapping research and complementary products, these five companies united in 1917 to form a new entity, the Union Carbide and Carbon Corporation. The search for other maverick talents attracted Union Carbide to Hugh S. Cooper, and KEMET was the result. **Ⓚ**

development of KEMET. The small firm was acquired by Union Carbide at a time when the great corporation was on an acquisitions tear, but unlike other organizations that came into Union Carbide in these years for their manufacturing or supply capabilities, KEMET was primarily a research and development lab. In effect, with KEMET, Union Carbide bought the company's brains — most notably, with Cooper serving as research director in Cleveland. Importantly, however, KEMET was not incorporated in Cleveland, but in Niagara Falls, NY, where another Union Carbide research operation, the Electro-Metallurgical Company, would help to shape its direction.

The Electro-Metallurgical Company was itself already a research and development company that had been founded by a man named Frederick Mark Becket (1875-1942). A Canadian trained at McGill University and Columbia University, Becket would later be described by one historian as "a metallurgical genius" who was responsible "for the greatest single contribution to American progress in alloys." And, like Cooper, Becket was ambitious. After briefly working for a metallurgical company in Niagara Falls, NY, he founded his own firm, Niagara Research Laboratories (1903), where he explored the use of silicon and ferrosilicon to reduce refractory ores, resulting in numerous patents. By using silicon instead of coke, Becket was able to produce a low-carbon ferrocarbon and a high chromium ferritic alloy that served as the essential ingredient for stainless steel. It was this work that made Edgar Price take notice when he organized the Electro-Metallurgical Company (1906) from a combination of Niagara Research Laboratories and a reorganized Willson Aluminum.

When KEMET was acquired by Union Carbide a few years later, Becket seemed a natural fit to oversee the new Cleveland-based research lab and help to coordinate its work with other divisions within the larger company. By this time, Union Carbide was large and growing more diffuse, with each new acquisition and attempted ntegration. For their part, Cooper and his colleagues prepared regular reports for Becket and his deputies at the Electro-Metallurgical Company, some of whom would occasionally shift from their regular assignments to support a KEMET project, as needed. In Cleveland, Cooper's indispensable right hand man was Maurice "Sarb" Sarbey (1887-1940), who served as chief engineer, first at Cooper Research Laboratories and throughout his time at KEMET.

FREDERICK MARK BECKET

(1875-1942)

"Frederick Mark Becket was — and is — a great soul."
-Transactions of the Electrochemical Society, 1942

Hailed as a "metallurgical genius," Becket oversaw research at KEMET during its first decade. Educated at McGill University and Columbia University, Becket had a distinguished career, working for several smaller firms before joining Union Carbide in 1906. He would serve as president or vice president of multiple divisions at the corporation, including the Electro-Metallurgical Company, Union Carbide Research Laboratories, and Haynes Stellite. His work developing electrothermic processes for reducing ores and producing alloys revolutionized commercial metallurgy. His innovations in the production of ferroalloys, particularly low-carbon ferrochromium, were vitally important in the industrial development of rustless iron and stainless steel. During World War I, he perfected zirconium steels used for light armor plate.

Becket was elected president of the American Electrochemical Society from 1925-1926, and president of the American Institute of Mining, Metallurgical, and Petroleum Engineers in 1933. He was lauded with the Perkins Medal for distinguished service in applied chemistry in 1924, the Edward Goodrich Acheson Medal from the Electrochemical Society in 1937, and the Elliott Cresson Medal from the Franklin Institute in 1940.[14] **K**

MAURICE D. SARBEY
(1887-1940)

Maurice "Sarb" Sarbey, KEMET's first engineer.

The engineer responsible for so many of KEMET's early successes was a man of many identities. Born in Russia in 1887, Morris Sarvinsky emigrated to the United States with his parents and older brothers in 1893. Yiddish was their first language. They settled in Akron, OH. By 1910, Morris had adopted the name Maurice Sarbinsky, which by 1920 he had shortened to Maurice Sarbey. His family called him Morris, and everyone at KEMET called him "Sarb."[15]

Sarb earned a B.S. in electrical engineering in 1911 from the Case School of Applied Science (later incorporated into Case Western University). Upon graduating he worked on a series of municipal projects, preparing plans and specifications for public utilities, subway stations, and buildings. A brilliant mechanic, Sarbey found more challenging work with Hugh Cooper, and together they worked as a team collaborating on many entrepreneurial ventures. Where Cooper developed the formulas, Sarbey designed and operated the specialized equipment they needed, and together they refined the processes that generated KEMET's early breakthroughs. Sarbey designed furnaces, induction regulators, an ammonia cracking system, cathodes, and getter assemblies for KEMET. He conducted metallurgical assays, and wrote most of the company's reports. When Cooper left KEMET in 1933, Sarbey went with him, serving as secretary, treasurer, and chief engineer of Cooper Products. He was renowned not only for his engineering skills but also for his wit — Sarbey wrote theatrical sketches and songs and published light verse in the *Cleveland Plain Dealer*.[16]

Now at Union Carbide, Sarbey and Cooper found themselves collaborating with other innovators within the larger firm. In 1925, for example, Sarbey developed an electric vacuum furnace, with an extremely effective seal, as well as novel components, such as a fitted microscope to allow for the measurement of critical points in alloys. The Sarbey Furnace was soon deployed across the divisions of Union Carbide and would later be improved by one of Becket's associates, Glen D. Bagley (1890-1969), with additional redesigns and more energy efficient processes. Although Bagley was based in New York and worked for Becket's Electro-Metallurgical Company, his patent was assigned to KEMET — a nod to the foundational work done by Sarbey and the people of KEMET.[17]

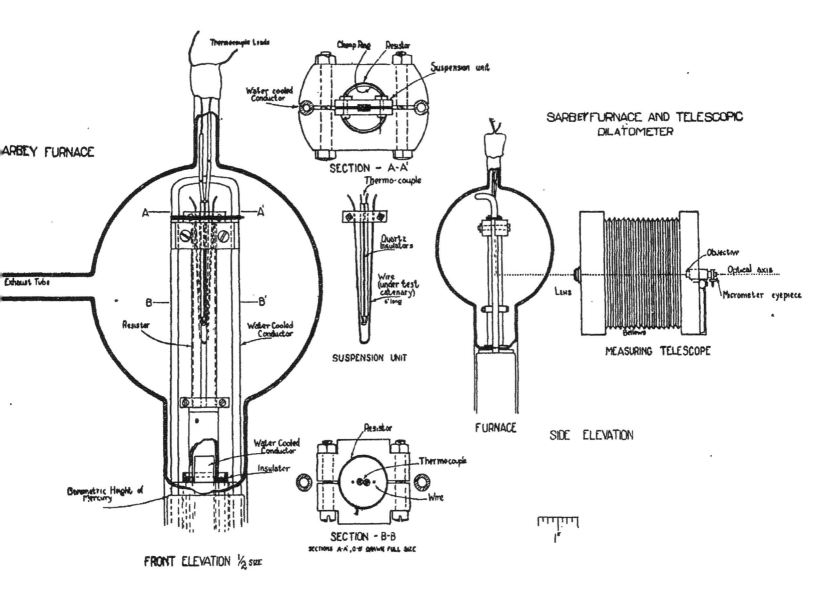

FIG. 1 — APPARATUS FOR DETERMINING CRITICAL POINTS OF WIRES

> *To investigate, experiment with, invent, discover and develop any and all metallurgical, electro-metallurgical, chemical, and electro-chemical products and compounds, including any and all substances and any and all alloys and compounds thereof; and any and all processes relating thereto.*

> – ARTICLES OF INCORPORATION
> *KEMET Laboratories Company, Inc., February 4, 1919.*

In its early years at Union Carbide, KEMET was a small research outfit. With a staff of fewer than ten people in the mid 1920s, Cooper, Sarbey, and their team of engineers, assistants, and one other chemist, initially focused on beryllium. It was the element that had fascinated Cooper for years, and now they went to work developing new methods to roll beryllium-aluminum alloys into sheets (in collaboration with Bell Labs). Because Union Carbide was not interested in launching an entirely new field of production, in 1924, the firm decided to sell the patents, and soon after Cooper patented a process for manufacturing beryllium in commercial quantities. In 1926 Percy Williams Bridgman, a professor of physics at Harvard and future Nobel Laureate, marveled at a sample rod of cast beryllium that Cooper sent, which was "apparently entirely free from inclusions of any kind."[18] The following year, Cooper, still every bit as commercially minded as he was chemically brilliant, engineered the sale of the patents to a venture capitalist in New York, Lester Hofheimer (1880-1936) and established the Beryllium Corporation of America (1927). It would be overseen by Cooper, Sarbey, and another key deputy, Menahem Merlub-Sobel (1900-1995). One of the first companies in the world to specialize in commercial production of the metal, the Beryllium Corporation could also produce its namesake at a rate that was a significant order of magnitude higher than anything achieved in earlier processes.[19]

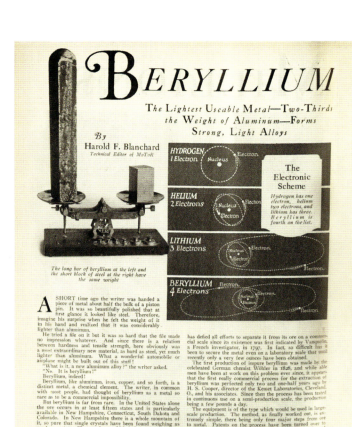

BERYLLIUM —the Wonder Metal

The Lightest Useable Metal—Two-Thirds the Weight of Aluminum—Forms Strong, Light Alloys

By
Harold F. Blanchard
Technical Editor of MoToR

The long bar of beryllium at the left and the short block of steel at the right have the same weight

The comparative size of beryllium and cast iron pistons both having the same weight is illustrated above. The smaller piston, of course, is cast iron

H. S. COOPER,
Director Kemet Laboratories, Inc., Cleveland, O., the first man to develop a fully commercial process for the extraction of beryllium

May 1928

30   MoToR   31

Above: Under Cooper, KEMET developed a revolutionary process for refining a rare metal. Their patents would become the foundation of a new company, the Beryllium Corporation of America.

Right: A patent memorandum relating to luminous paint signed by Cooper and witnessed by his deputies, 1933.

Meanwhile, KEMET continued to focus on diverse areas of research. Despite the team's small size, they made critical discoveries and filed patents associated with rare materials and a range of components.[20] Cooper also tried his hand at tantalum, the element that would become the company's

continued on page 28

PIGMENT MEMORANDUM

LUMINOUS PLASTICS

The invention relates to solid bodies luminous in the dark, which are inert to moisture and other atmospheric influences, and which can be machined and worked into various commercial shapes.

The product of this invention is made up of the natural or synthetic resins or plastics and a luminous pigment. Typical organic materials which are suitable for acting as a pigment base are the vinyl group, a commercial product of this group being known as "vinylite", and the urea-formaldehyde resins, formerly known as pollopas. The resins to be mixed with the pigment should preferably be colorless or only faintly tinted in order that the product shall develop the maximum phosphorescent qualities. Cellulose abstate or other similar cellulose compounds may also be used as a base for the pigment.

The pigment itself may consist of a luminous sulphide made up of zinc, calcium, barium, strontium, magnesium or mixtures of these luminous bodies, and may be blended in finely divided form with the powdered resins after which the mixture is compressed into the desired forms under heat. Products are suitable for making luminous signs, electric push buttons, night stands and other products of similar nature which are required to luminesce in the dark.

Sept. 27, 1933.

Sept. 26, 1933

Two views (above and right) of the key element of the furnace Maurice Sarbey designed to determine critical points in chromium-iron alloys. Note the lab reports hanging in the background of the picture on the right.

Cooper was first and foremost a chemist. In the mid 1920s, his lab on the second floor of 4503 Euclid Avenue in Cleveland, was filled with the materials necessary for the company's investigations of compounds of beryllium, thorium, zirconium, and other rare metals. Even when KEMET's focus shifted to perfecting elements of radio and vacuum tubes, Cooper experimented with enamels, paint pigments, and other fields of electrochemistry.

Left: Much of KEMET's efforts in the early years was devoted to developing methods for producing beryllium on a commercial scale. First, beryl ore was fed into a crusher (the small machine to the right of trays of ore) and then ground into a powder. The powder was mixed with chemicals to promote decomposition and fusion and placed in a furnace enclosed behind a heavy door to contain the heat. The fluid result was processed to produce beryllium oxide, which could then be further refined.

KEMET used this equipment to refine metals, including beryllium, thorium, and barium, through electrolysis. Right: Materials, including powdered metals, water, acids, and binding agents, depending upon the desired results, were introduced from the upper units to the large wooden tank in the foreground. The tap at the base of the tank was used to sample the chemical composition of the slurry within. Above: A set of stairs gave technicians access to the upper tanks. Two banks of filters drew off the precipitated compound, which would be further processed in a furnace or crucible.

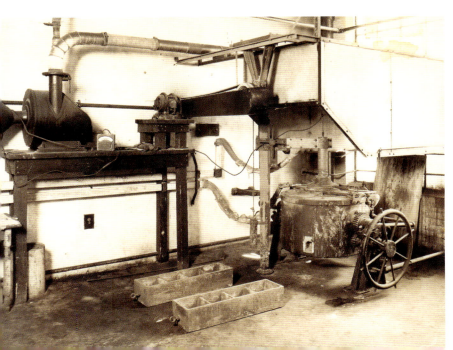

A crucible with a graphite electrode, used for producing beryllium and ferroalloys. The unit worked at high temperatures, probably between 1300°-1800°C. The funnel on the left served as a filter pump to draw in air, the hood above the unit exhausted fumes. The small opening at the bottom of the crucible allowed the product to flow out into molds, two of which are on the floor.

Left: A furnace for casting alkaline earth metals in a purified condition. Gas was introduced to drive out air and increase pressure. Material was pumped in through the pipe at the left and poured out through the funnel on the right. Note the ropes used to adjust the position of the furnace. The vertical steel tubes in the background served as a particle separator to precipitate oxides, nitrides, hydrides, which are produced through the combination of metals and gases.

KEMET's first power plant, including a transformer and a rectifier, used to convert the current needed to run the machinery and catalyze the company's electrometallurgical processes.

MENAHEM MERLUB-SOBEL
(1900-1995)

Born in Brooklyn, NY, Merlub-Sobel received both an engineering degree and a master's degree from Columbia University in 1924. He moved to Cleveland to pursue doctoral studies at Western Reserve University (now Case Western University), and started work at the Warner Chemical Company, which produced soap. Cooper recognized his potential and hired the young scientist in 1925 to help set up the Beryllium Corporation of America. In 1926, he brought him back to KEMET Laboratories to work on other projects, and it was while at KEMET that Merlub-Sobel completed his dissertation on the electrodeposition of metals in andydrous ammonia. In 1931, Merlub Sobel returned to the Beryllium Corporation, and then went on to have a long and distinguished career in research and teaching, including a stint, shortly after Israeli independence, as the chair of the Department of Chemical Engineering at Technion: Israel Institute of Technology. His 1944 handbook of metals and alloys was for many years considered an essential reference.[21] **K**

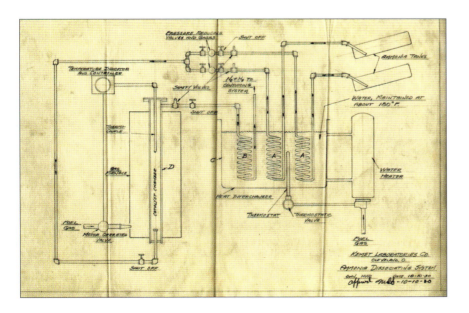

Top: Merlub-Sobel, pictured in 1950. Bottom: Sarbey's plan for apparatus designed by Merlub-Sobel to break ammonia into its component parts, hydrogen and nitrogen.

Scientific staff at another division of Union Carbide, the Electro-Metallurgical Company, worked closely with personnel at KEMET. Among those pictured is Glen D. Bagley (#4), who worked with Sarbey on improving a vacuum furnace on getters, Thomas Cunningham (#6), worked with Robert Price at KEMET on the separation of tantalum from columbium (niobium). In turn, Cooper refined columbium in exchange for work on stainless steel by Becket and Russell Franks (#1).

most important material after 1960. A hard metal, tantalum is always found in the presence of another element, columbium (now called niobium), which needs to be separated from tantalum. The process of separating tantalum from niobium would occupy Cooper and his colleagues at Union Carbide for many years. The result would prove critical not only for KEMET but also for the work of Becket and Russell Franks at Electro-Metallurgical Company on chromium steels.[22]

Ultimately, however, it was not beryllium or tantalum that would be most important to KEMET's early fortunes, but another element entirely: barium. Beginning around 1925, George Choate Furness (1884-1944), a Massachusetts Institute of Technology (MIT) trained physicist who had worked alongside Becket at Electro-Metallurgical Company and who was now the director of Union Carbide's Eveready battery division, suggested that KEMET pursue something new: getters for vacuum tubes. In collaboration with Furness, Cooper and Sarbey turned their attention to materials that might help to absorb the residual gases produced inside a vacuum tube. These absorption materials were known as 'getters,' and, with the rise of radio and other emergent technologies, any breakthrough in the field that could increase the efficiency and longevity of a vacuum tube might also have significant commercial potential. That the inspiration for KEMET's focus on getters came from elsewhere at Union Carbide was indicative of the larger company's efforts to promote the free flow of ideas and innovations across divisions, particularly in research and development. What happened next — a breakthrough with barium and the unlocking of the potential in vacuum tubes — would not only transform the company, but also position KEMET to revolutionize the entire field of electronics.

George C. Furness, the manager of Eveready asked KEMET to develop a better getter.

CHAPTER TWO:

PERFECTING THE VACUUM

THE RISE OF THE VACUUM TUBE, THE DEVELOPMENT OF ADVANCED ELECTRONICS, AND the rise of KEMET went hand in hand. The period from 1925 to 1955 saw extraordinary advances in technology — radios became popular and inexpensive, X-ray machines became safer, oscilloscopes became viable, and the world witnessed the birth of miraculous new machines: industrial control systems, television, radar, and computers. These advances all relied upon the vacuum tube, today regarded as a quaint and antiquated device, but back then the heart and soul of cutting edge developments in electronics. The first vacuum tubes were unreliable, limited in power, and burned out quickly. What made them work was a deceptively simple little device made by KEMET.

KEMET's getters served to remove the last vestiges of gas from an electron tube, creating as perfect a vacuum as possible. With the residual gases removed, vacuum tubes were rendered more reliable, more powerful, and more durable. This allowed for the development of increasingly sophisticated electronics. The vacuum tube was perhaps the single most important component responsible for launching the technological breakthroughs of the first half of the twentieth century, and KEMET made it happen.

If the vacuum tube was the egg that hatched the electronic miracles of the 1930s and 1940s, the radio was the chicken, and in this case the chicken came first. Radio was the most fundamental invention of the electronic age; one can draw a direct line of development from the radio to the computer and beyond. The first patents for "wireless telegraphs" were granted in the early 1870s. Thomas Edison, Alexander Graham Bell, and Nikola Tesla made significant improvements to communications in the 1880s and 1890s. Ferdinand Braun then made a crucial breakthrough with his invention of the closed circuit system. However, it was Guglielmo Marconi building on experiments by James Clerk Maxwell and Heinrich Hertz on radio waves, who developed the first practical radio communication system in 1897.

The first radios depended on primitive technology like spark gap transmitters, arc converters, and Alexanderson alternators. The first transatlantic radio transmission in 1901 required the construction of an enormous spark transmitter powered by a 25 kilowatt alternator driven by a combustion engine. Radio receivers were built around crystal detectors — a simple device whose most essential elements were a small crystal (usually galena or pyrite) and a thin "whisker" wire connected to a coil of wire that served as a tuner. Crystal radio sets were cheap and easy to construct, though limited in their function: the power was too low to use a loudspeaker, so headphones were required to listen.

Radio's popularity drove innovation. In 1904, Marconi's associate Alexander Fleming invented the thermionic vacuum tube in an effort to improve reception. Soon, the device would render earlier radio apparatus obsolete, and open up a whole new world of possibility. But before that could happen, the structure of the industry had to change. Through the 1910s, Marconi's Wireless Company held most of the key patents on radio technology. But Marconi was a British company, and during the early years of WWI, England and the United States had clashed, with the British going so far as to sever the telegraph cable that connected America to Europe.

1883
Thomas Edison invents the "electrical indicator," the precursor to the vacuum tube.

1915
Irving Langmuir (above at left) at General Electric invents the first getter, a device for removing gases from a vacuum tube.

1927
In response to a request from the Eveready division of Union Carbide, Cooper and Sarbey develop the barium getter.

1928
Vladimir K. Zworykin at Westinghouse invents the iconoscope, the first television photo tube.

1933
KEMET shifts its primary focus from R&D to manufacturing. Its getters will soon be featured in virtually every vacuum tube manufactured in the United States and England.

1939-1946
KEMET's workforce triples as the company produces getters for vacuum tubes needed during WWII.

1947-1954
KEMET's workforce doubles again to meet the demand for getters for cathode tubes used in a rapidly growing television market.

THE RADIO AT WAR

At first, the wireless radio transmitter was initially used only by naval stations in the United States and England for communications from ship to ship and between ship and shore. For the first time one could contact a ship without worrying about fog, darkness, or precise location. Radio spread to civilian uses with

Field communication equipment during the early stages of WWI was so bulky it had to be transported by horse.

the first broadcast in 1906, and the first radio stations were established around 1908, but for the first decade or so, the invention was used primarily by a relatively small network of amateur enthusiasts who built their own crystal radio sets. The outbreak of WWI (1914-1918) altered this virtually overnight. In the conflicts of the latter half of the nineteenth century, communications specialists laid down telegraph wires as fast as possible. But radio was wireless. Instant radio communications provided an immediate tactical advantage in the first global conflict. As one journalist noted, "a very large number of young men, who in days gone by took their initial steps in radio training as amateurs, have now proved the value of their hobby, and today are performing useful service *pro patria*."[1] By the end of the war, radio technology had advanced to the point that bulky "portable" transmitters — so large that they had to be brought to the field on horses — were routinely outfitted on vehicles, ships, and planes. The needs of the armed forces had changed the status of radio communications from novelty to necessity. During the 1920s, the new technology would spread from the fields of battle to the living rooms of middle class homes across the world. By the 1930s and 1940s, they were cheap enough so that most families could afford one. **K**

After the war, Franklin Delano Roosevelt, then assistant secretary of the Navy, joined with Owen D. Young of General Electric (GE) to organize a joint venture that would consolidate American research in wireless communications and break the Marconi Company monopoly. They compelled the Marconi Company to sell its American subsidiary to GE, which partnered with American Telephone and Telegraph (AT&T) and Westinghouse to form the Radio Corporation of America (RCA). The amalgamation of these technology pioneers into a unified cartel made possible the advanced development of the vacuum tube. As one historian has noted, "The vacuum tube, more than any other single feature in the progress of radio, required a mass attack on its theory, its mathematics, its construction and its behavior; and this was not made until the laboratories of the great corporations had turned their attention to the problem."[2]

Dr. Irving Langmuir (left) and Guglielmo Marconi at General Electric Laboratories, 1922.

the Magic Brain of all
electronic equipment
is a tube . . .

Before the invention of the transistor, vacuum tubes — also called electron tubes or valves — operated as switches and amplifiers in complex elecctronic equipment, including radios, radars, and early computers.

VACUUM TUBES AND GETTERS

At its most basic, the vacuum tube controls the flow of electric current between two electrodes. In an early configuration (called *the diode*), a tube consisted of two elements: a heated cathode and a cold anode. The addition of a third element, a grid, allowed for the amplification and control of current via a *triode*. Although this would become the foundation of all electronic circuitry during the first half of the twentieth century, early triode vacuum tubes were highly unstable, burning out quickly. In the early 1910s, Harold D. Arnold, a young physicist at AT&T, pinpointed the problem: the ionization of gases inside the tube. Improving the vacuum would make vacuum tubes more effective and longer lasting. At the time, this was counterintuitive, because conventional wisdom held that gases were necessary to transport electrons from one element to the other. Nevertheless, at AT&T, Arnold began experimenting with oxides as a means of removing gases. Meanwhile, a theoretical chemist at GE named Irving Langmuir reached a similar conclusion, and the race was on. In 1913, Langmuir designed the first "getter" as a complicated series of chambers, one of which held an alkali metal (such as potassium), to absorb trace gases.[3] But there was always room for improvement, and with such high stakes, research at GE and AT&T overlapped so frequently that between 1912 and 1926 there were more than 20 patent interferences between the two companies.[4] KEMET's invention of the barium getter changed the game, producing results far superior to anything that had been developed earlier, and setting the standard for decades to come. **Ⓚ**

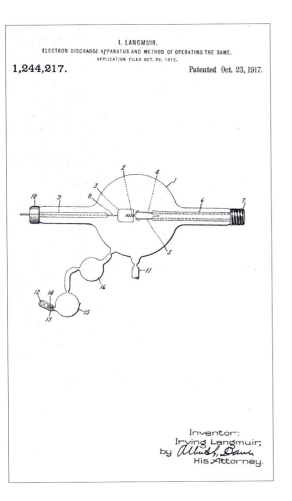

I. LANGMUIR.
ELECTRON DISCHARGE APPARATUS AND METHOD OF OPERATING THE SAME.
APPLICATION FILED OCT. 28. 1915.

1,244,217.

Patented Oct. 23, 1917.

Inventor:
Irving Langmuir,
by *Albert G. Davis*
His Attorney.

The first getters were conceived as a series of chambers that would draw off residual gases. KEMET's solution was simpler and more efficient.

Through GE, RCA controlled a host of patents on covering virtually every aspect of radio technology, from broadcasting towers to vacuum tubes. Rather than freezing other companies out of the industry, RCA licensed the rights to manufacture parts and components on a non-exclusive basis. By licensing its patents, RCA not only reaped extraordinary dividends, they also kept control of technological standards, ensuring that every other radio company would manufacture parts according to the specifications that RCA established. RCA collected royalties on every vacuum tube sold by over a dozen companies, each of which sold millions of tubes each year.[5]

One of RCA's licensees was the Eveready Battery Company, a subsidiary of Union Carbide. Eveready had begun life with a narrow range of specialization (flashlights and the batteries that powered them). By the late 1910s, they had a rapidly expanding product line, at the top of which were battery-powered radios, particularly popular in areas that had not yet been wired for electricity. In 1923, the company launched *The Eveready Hour*, the first major variety show ever broadcast. On the show, noted one historian of old time radio "a farmer in distant Pennsylvania could

PATENTS UNDER WHICH RCA GRANTS LICENSES COVERING A TYPICAL RADIO BROADCAST RECEIVER TUBE *

DOME SHAPE BULB TUBE
1 PATENT

CARBON COATED BULB
1 PATENT

GRID
2 PATENTS

GETTER
5 PATENTS

TIPLESS STEM
1 PATENT

ANODE
6 PATENTS

CATHODE
10 PATENTS

ELECTRODE ASSEMBLY
20 PATENTS

DUMET LEAD
1 PATENT

OCTAL BASE
1 PATENT

Licensing patents served as a major source of income for RCA and other companies operating in a highly competitive electronics marketplace.

George Furness, who steered KEMET towards its work on getters, hosted the first variety show on radio.

experience what had, until then, been the exclusive province of cosmopolites."[6] Monologues by Will Rogers, performances by George Gershwin, and dramatizations of Shakespeare were now widely available. The host of the show was none other than George Choate Furness (1884-1944), manager of the Eveready division at Union Carbide, and one of the earliest directors at KEMET.

At Union Carbide, Furness was part of a tight band of scientist managers linked by academic and personal ties. This included William J. Knapp, the first president of KEMET, who was in Furness' class at MIT and was not incidentally the son of Union Carbide's CEO. James H. Critchett was another MIT alum and director of research at KEMET, and Paul P. Huffard was Furness' brother-in-law who served later as a director at KEMET and a vice president at Union Carbide.[7] Each of these men shared common academic, intellectual, and personal bonds, which allowed them to streamline operations between KEMET and the other divisions at Union Carbide.[8]

This is precisely why George C. Furness thought to write to Hugh Cooper and his associates to ask about improving the thermionic tube. KEMET had developed a reputation for successful experimentation with rare metals, and although Cooper remained passionate about his breakthroughs with beryllium, company directors were losing interest. In 1925, Cooper began work on alloys of thorium, an element used in radio filaments. He soon produced a thorium-tungsten alloy that was so superior to the more widely used thorium-oxide filaments that GE offered $250,000 (over $3.5 million in 2019 dollars) to purchase the invention for RCA. KEMET's parent company, Union Carbide, declined. It was a missed opportunity, Cooper later recalled, "The failure to dispose of these patents proved to be poor judgment on the part of the company officials, because not long thereafter, oxide coated filamentary bodies became standard throughout the entire radio tube industry and replaced completely the thoriated tungsten type of wire." [9]

Meanwhile, KEMET research advanced on other, related fronts. Maurice "Sarb" Sarbey, for example, focused on processes for engineering thermionic tubes and patented an improvement to the design of the cathode. [10] In 1926, Furness raised the bar, asking Sarbey to develop radio tubes that would meet higher specifications than any that had previously existed:

Filament volts	*1*
Filament amperes	*2*
Amplification constant	*5*
Plate voltage about	*200*

…Filament to be short and stocky, about 1" long, of the "straight thru" type…

"Our previous experience has been largely in duplicating existing tubes rather than in designing new types," Sarbey wrote in his response, "consequently we had to do considerable experimenting." [11]

Before settling on getters, KEMET scientists experimented with a variety of improvements to vacuum tubes.

Coming up with a new vacuum tube was an ambitious initiative that also proved to be short lived. Furness came to realize that KEMET's core capabilities in the early years of the 1920s were better focused on the development of alloys. Instead, Union Carbide forged a partnership with a new company that already had some experience with tubes but was struggling to survive in RCA's shadow. That young company was Raytheon, and although Eveready-Raytheon tubes were marketed for only a few years, the relationship forged between the two companies would endure through the decades.[12]

Union Carbide's cooperative venture with Raytheon depended on KEMET getters.

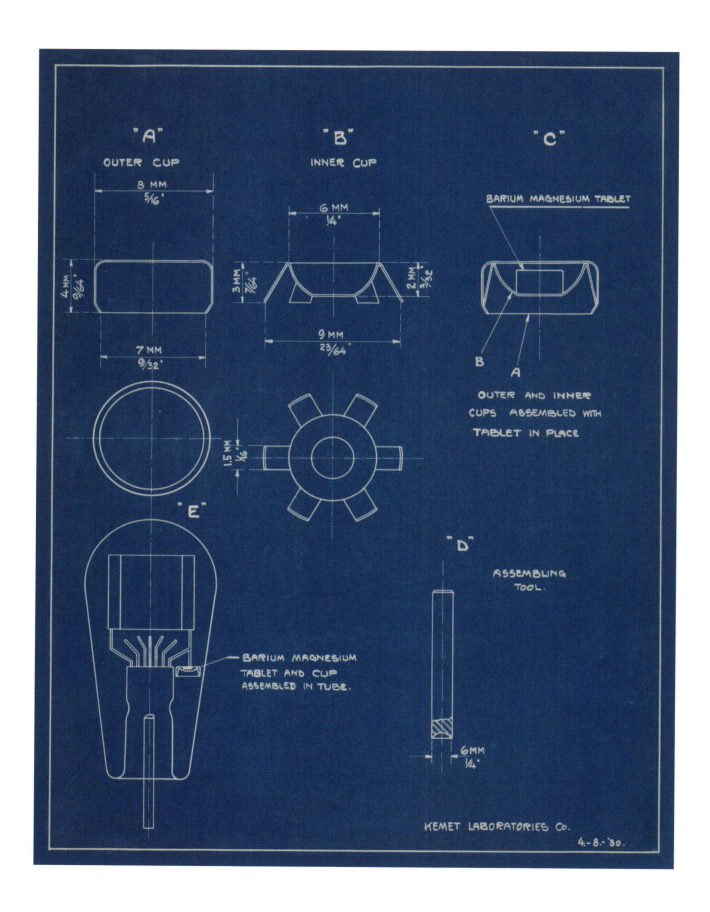

KEMET scientists may have stepped away from the construction of tubes more generally, but their work on the component parts of vacuum tubes was making steady progress. Then, in 1926 — a breakthrough. Amid a background of legal disputes over general vacuum tube patents, the race was still on for the most precise method to produce the best vacuum. By the 1920s, pumps were used inside vacuum tubes to extract most of the air during manufacture. Next, a cleanup chemical agent was added, and a pellet was placed on a small mount within the tube that would react with residual gases. The agent was heated up (in a process called "flashing"), and the resulting chemical reaction created a solid that coated the interior of the tube. This process was called "fixing." At KEMET, Cooper and his team discovered that a compound of barium oxide (BaO, initially mixed with magnesium and later strontium and aluminum) produced the best results.[13]

This new getter represented a pivotal discovery, with immediate implications for the radio industry. RCA's licensing system maintained a high level of standardization in the industry, so any significant improvement to a fundamental component would swiftly ripple throughout the entire industry. A better getter meant a more powerful, reliable, and durable vacuum tube. Within a decade of Cooper's discovery, KEMET would dominate the market for getters. But this did not happen overnight; it took some years before the company was retooled to capitalize on its most significant product.

The delay was due to the fact that KEMET was then first and foremost a research lab, not a manufacturing plant. The company produced getters, but only on a relatively small scale. Meanwhile, Cooper and Sarbey continued their research on other components of the vacuum tube, working on filaments, for example, and molybdenum wire, used for grids within vacuum tubes. But they never fully confined their focus to the vacuum tube, however important it might be. Cooper's interests were wide ranging, pursuing projects that were homegrown, as well as others that came down from his superiors at Union Carbide. In response to a request from Frederick M. Becket, for example, Cooper worked on refining niobium (then called columbium) for use in the production of stainless steel. Cooper and his team also developed an apparatus for disassociating

Opposite: KEMET's first getters took the form of pellets placed in a small receptacle. Later the company would develop specialized assemblies.

(or "cracking") ammonia (NH_3) into Hydrogen (H_2) and Nitrogen (N_2) for the Linde Air Company, as well as a process for melting. One of Cooper's assistants, Robert C. Price, collaborated with Thomas R. Cunningham, a scientist at Union Carbide's lab in Long Island City, NY, on a process for separating tantalum from niobium. Glidden, then the largest paint company in the world, was located nearby in Cleveland, and Cooper began to map out experiments for improving pigments and varnishes.[14]

The stock market crash of 1929 hit the economy hard, but radio sales remained strong.

As the 1920s came to a close, the ground at KEMET began to shift. First came the stock market crash in October 1929, which plunged the United States and much of the world into an economic depression that would drag on for years. (Though radios, which offered reprieve from the pressures of the day, would continue to sell steadily throughout the period.) Then, in 1931, Frederick M. Becket was promoted to vice president at Union Carbide and left his duties at the Electro Metallurgical Company to become president of the Union Carbide and Carbon Research Laboratories Inc. James A. Holladay, one of Becket's deputies stepped in as president of KEMET Laboratories. Under new management, the company would shift from pure research to manufacturing.

At the time, KEMET was operating at a significant loss. In the first quarter of 1930, for example, the labs expenses were $77,318.13 (about $1.16 million in 2019 dollars), including over $33,700 for lab equipment, $23,000 for research expenses, and $17,500 for manufacturing operations. Major research was ongoing in four areas: (1) tungsten and molybdenum, (2) tantalum and niobium, (3) barium and related products, and (4) what Cooper and Sarbey named, perhaps appropriately, "other problems." The lab sold five products: barium metal, barium-magnesium tablets, copper-clad barium pellets, tungsten and molybdenum wire, and "miscellaneous." Total income from sales: just over $29,500. Some products sold well and at good margins, such as barium getters, which tallied expenses of around $9,000 to produce revenue of approximately $25,000 (approximately $444,000 in 2019 dollars). Molybdenum wire, on the other hand, was produced and sold at a loss. At KEMET, Sarbey acknowledged that although KEMET's molybdenum wire was inferior to other products on the market, "the demand for wire was so great that customers were not critical and were glad to buy it." The rationale for continuing to churn out some substandard products alongside cutting-edge technologies was that at a certain volume KEMET would be able to make the wire profitably. By July 1931, this still worked only in theory, however — not in practice.[15]

In these difficult years, KEMET depended on Union Carbide. If not for the larger organization, KEMET almost certainly would have been forced to close its doors. It was only with the financial and managerial commitment of KEMET's parent company that Cooper's research outfit weathered the challenges of the financial crash. Union Carbide was committed to investing in research and development, with an awareness that short-term losses were the cost of profitable breakthroughs. Still, even for an organization as committed to a long-term vision as Union Carbide, these were trying times, and they demanded tough decisions. From his office in New York, Holladay, as the new president of KEMET, began to rein in KEMET's operations. Questionable lines of inquiry were abandoned, as Cooper and Sarbey refocused on vacuum tubes, and barium getters in particular. At the National Carbon complex at 117th Street and Madison Avenue in Lakewood, OH, near Cleveland, KEMET designed and supervised the construction of units capable of producing barium and strontium on a commercial scale.[16]

From 1933 to 1971, KEMET operated out of the National Carbon complex in Lakewood, OH.

This shift may have kept KEMET alive, but it also stifled the company's entrepreneurial founder. Cooper had a passion for research and invention. It was never enough for him to focus on discoveries that could incrementally improve existing technologies for the sake of the bottom line. From the start, he was an inventor. As KEMET's focus changed during the Great Depression, Cooper privately complained to his colleagues, until, in 1933, he finally broke his association with Union Carbide. Under the terms of the split, Cooper agreed to keep the lab he had long occupied at 4501 Euclid Avenue, taking Sarbey and several other staff with him. KEMET's name and patents, however, remained with Union Carbide. Reincorporating as Cooper Products, Inc., Cooper and Sarbey went on to work on the manufacture of beryllium alloys, a process for coating steel with chromium, lubricants made of molybdenum sulfide, and numerous other chemical and metallurgical projects.

Not everyone left KEMET when Cooper and Union Carbide parted ways, however. Other important members of the team opted to remain. Chief among these was John D. McQuade (1896-1980), who worked with Cooper both on getters and on molybdenum wire. As a researcher, McQuade did not share Cooper's wide-ranging interests. The five patents registered under his name between 1933 and 1942 were all narrowly focused on improving the operation of vacuum tubes.[17] While Cooper was a passionate inventor and entrepreneur, always working to develop a product or a process that could be sold for other firms to develop, McQuade was methodical in his approach, practical, and market-driven. McQuade and his superiors at Union Carbide understood the lesson articulated by Raytheon's co-founder Vannevar Bush. Cooper's genius was in invention; McQuade's was in development.

Strong organizational support was key to McQuade's success. The structure of Union Carbide, which included 10 laboratories across its various divisions even during the depths of the Great Depression.

> *An invention is valueless unless it is joined with a number of other accomplishments – promotion, financing, development, engineering, marketing, and so on.*
>
> – *Vannevar Bush*
> *RAYTHEON*[18]

Personnel at National Carbon, Lakewood, OH, 1935.

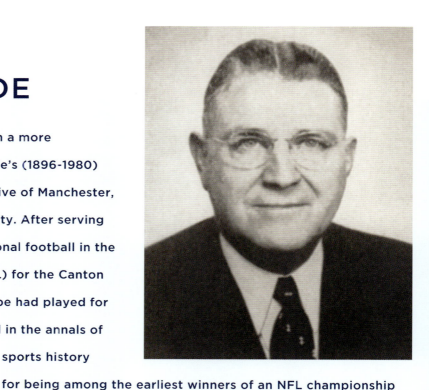

JOHN D. MCQUADE

Unlike most of his colleagues who came from a more traditional, scientific tracks, John D. McQuade's (1896-1980) journey to KEMET was an unusual one. A native of Manchester, NH, McQuade attended Georgetown University. After serving in the Army during WWI, he played professional football in the newly formed National Football League (NFL) for the Canton Bulldogs, the same team Olympian Jim Thorpe had played for just a few years earlier. McQuade is recorded in the annals of sports history for being among the earliest winners of an NFL championship in 1922. McQuade might have continued his career in football but the opportunity was abruptly whisked away. In 1924, the owner of the NFL's Cleveland Indians bought the Canton Bulldogs on an impulse and moved them to Cleveland. He then had second thoughts, tried to resell the team, and then simply disbanded it. In short order, McQuade found himself in a strange city and out of a job. Fortunately, he had connections. In 1923, he had married Ruth Furness, the younger sister of George Furness (director of Eveready) and Helen Furness (wife of Union Carbide executive Paul P. Huffard). Now, McQuade's brothers-in-law welcomed him into the family business. It was a fortuitous circumstance all around. Under McQuade, KEMET would prosper. **K**

Union Carbide's research labs included KEMET, the Electro-Metallurgical Company, the Haynes Stellite Company, the Linde Air Products Company, the National Carbon Company, and Prest-O-Lite. In addition to these divisional labs focused on improving products, Union Carbide maintained two research labs, the largest of which, in Long Island City, NY, had about 100 metallurgists, electrical, mechanical, and mining engineers, physicists, chemists, and other scientists on staff. Overlapping leadership pyramids encouraged lateral communications and collaboration between divisions. For example, while John McQuade served as director of KEMET, James A. Holladay served as president of KEMET and director of the Electro-Metallurgical Company's laboratories in Niagara Falls, NY. James H. Critchett (1886-1957), a vice president of Union Carbide, was also executive officer in charge of research at KEMET, the Electro-Metallurgical Company, the Haynes Stellite Company, and Union Carbide.[19]

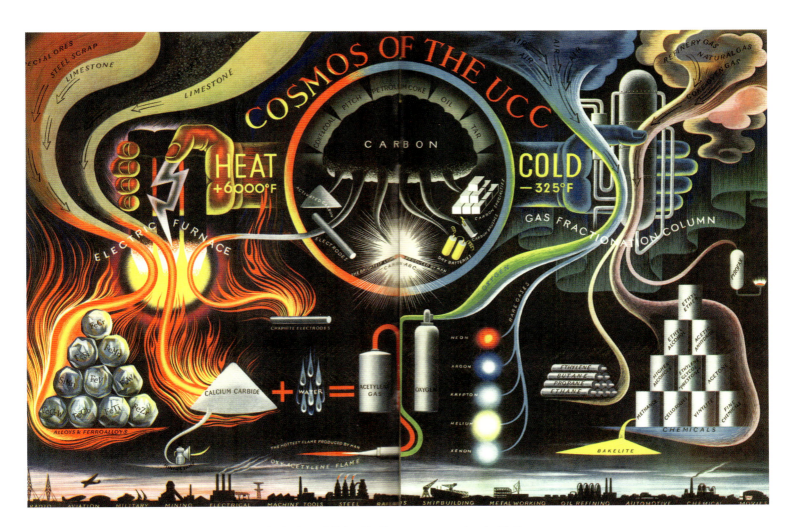

An artist's rendition of the scope of Union Carbide published in Fortune magazine in 1941.

JAMES H. CRITCHETT

James H. Critchett (1886-1957) was one of the scientifically trained managers whose oversight was key to KEMET's early success. Born in Watertown, MA, he attended MIT in neighboring Cambridge, writing a thesis on the electrical conductivity of carbon and graphite at high temperatures. His leadership potential was recognized early on when his college peers elected him president of the senior class.[20] His first management positions were in the steel industry. He worked at U.S. Steel in Chicago, helping to install one of the first large electric steel furnaces to be erected in America. In 1912, he moved to Michigan to work with the Buchanan Electric Street Company. In 1915, he joined Electro-Metallugical Company to serve as assistant to Frederick M. Becket. He would spend the rest of his long career directing research at Union Carbide.

When KEMET was organized in 1919, Critchett served as an assistant to the board. In 1921, Union Carbide established its important research laboratory in Long Island City, NY, bringing together top talent from each of the corporation's divisions. Critchett served as manager of the Metallurgical Division. In 1930, he would later be promoted to vice president of the Research Division. In 1935, he was elected president of the Electrochemical Society. When the United States entered WWII, he served his country by sitting on the committee on metallurgy of the War Production Board, ensuring that the U.S. Armed Forces were supplied with the materials they needed. He retired from his duties at KEMET — and Union Carbide — shortly after the war. **K**

"There's a dollar sign in front of everything we do," James Critchett told *Fortune* magazine. Together, he, Holladay, and McQuade reinvented KEMET, with a focus on profitability. Because Cooper kept the research labs he had so long occupied, the company moved to the National Carbon complex, which occupied several blocks along Madison Avenue in Lakewood, OH, with a laboratory and factory at one end (117th Street) and administrative offices at the other (119th Street). No longer a freewheeling research laboratory, KEMET was reimagined as a manufacturing plant with a highly active R&D program. In a 1933 directory of industrial research, KEMET described its agenda in Cooper's terms:

> *Full time [research] on unusual refractories such as thoria, beryllia, zirconia, etc., preparation of so-called rare metals – zirconium, beryllium and thorium and investigation of alloys of these metals, radio and vacuum tube work and high emission filaments, enamel opacifying media and paint pigments, etc., electroplating of rare metals.*
>
> *– KEMET, 1933*

Just a little over a decade later, a new research profile was presented to position KEMET in the 1946 edition of the same directory:

> *The creation of new, and the improvement of present, getters and grid wires for radio tubes and other electronic devices, technical consultation and service with customers.*
>
> *– KEMET, 1946*

On January 1, 1950, Union Carbide took the transition even further. KEMET, which in 1919 had been officially named "Kemet Laboratories Company, Inc." was now redesignated "the Kemet Division" of Union Carbide.[21]

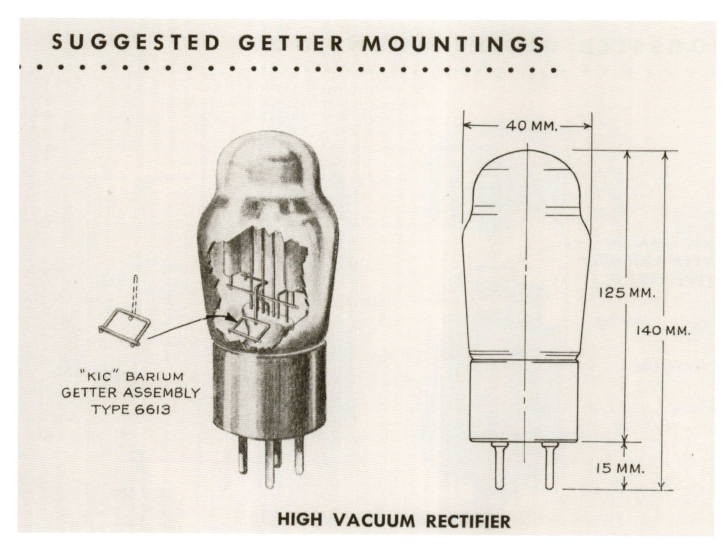

SUGGESTED GETTER MOUNTINGS

"KIC" BARIUM
GETTER ASSEMBLY
TYPE 6613

40 MM.

125 MM.

140 MM.

15 MM.

HIGH VACUUM RECTIFIER

Above: One of the many varieties of KIC getter assemblies KEMET sold in 1948.

Right: KEMET getter, activated with induction coil, 1940. The dark patches in the activated tubes are created by the chemical reaction of barium with residual gases in the tubes. They are a sign that the process worked.

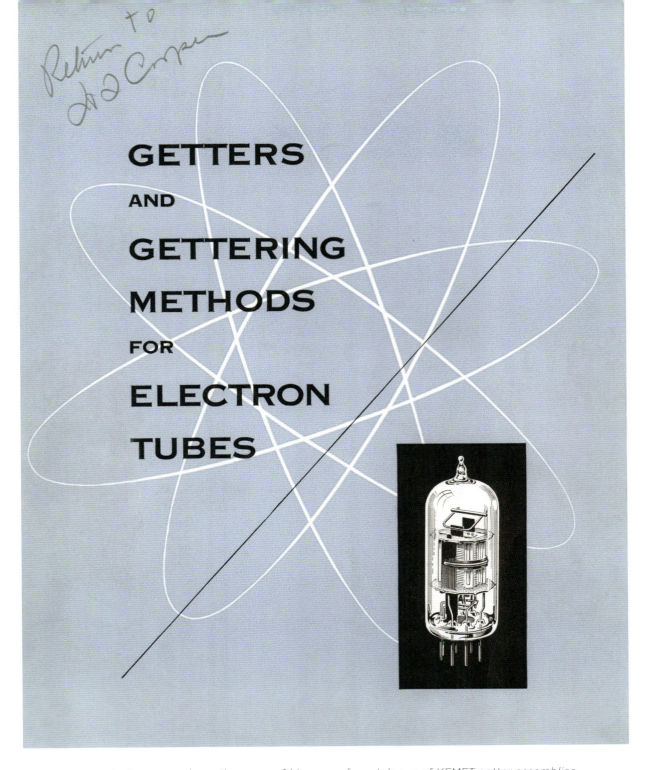

GETTERS

AND

GETTERING

METHODS

FOR

ELECTRON

TUBES

Hugh S. Cooper's signature adorns the cover of his copy of a catalogue of KEMET getter assemblies from the mid 1940s. Although he was no longer at the company at that point, he took great pride in its continuing success.

Under the leadership of Critchett, Holladay, and McQuade, KEMET was retooled from an R&D lab to a getter factory, with a dramatically increased production capacity. The first barium getters at KEMET consisted of a pellet placed in a tiny cup (later called a "flag," made of nickel) within the tube. Later, KEMET developed getter assemblies in a wide range of styles to be mounted within tubes produced by a range of manufacturers. Marketed under the name KIC (KEMET Iron Clad), these getter assemblies included a barium core protected by an iron sheath to form a bar that was then welded across a nickel wire bent into a U shape to form a closed loop, which could then be mounted in the tube.

Many businesses suffered after the stock market crash in 1929. By 1933, 25 percent of the American workforce was unemployed. Although people struggled economically, radio sales remained steady. In fact, radio is widely credited with helping people survive the challenges of the Great Depression. A growing number of entertainment programs — comedies, dramas, mysteries, music, and variety shows — offered a much needed escape from life's daily pressures. Most important, perhaps, were the Fireside Chats that President Franklin Delano Roosevelt broadcast each week to inform the

Radio offered comfort to people struggling to make ends meet during the Great Depression.

public and reassure listeners that however bleak the day, the future remained bright. In the 1920s, radios were a luxury item. In the 1930s, they became a daily necessity, and most households found the means to buy one. In 1922, 100,000 radio sets were produced in the United States, with 1 million vacuum tubes manufactured. By 1933, annual production hit 3.8 million radios and 59 million vacuum tubes. By 1941, the last year of the economic crisis, manufacturers produced 13 million radios and 130 million vacuum tubes annually.[22]

KEMET getter assemblies were a mainstay of the division's success during the Great Depression and would prove critical during World War II. Not only were radio communications vital in military operations, but an entirely new technology had arisen that would increase demand: radar. As with the radio, radar technology depended on specialized vacuum tubes, which meant that KEMET's getters would be indispensable.

Invented in the late 1930s, radar (an acronym for RAdio Detection And Ranging) gave British and American ships and planes a considerable advantage in combat, and proved crucial to the Allied war effort. As a nascent technology, however, the production of radar devices placed heavy demands on manufacturers. Between 1943 and 1944 the demand for airborne radio equipment rose nearly 250 percent. Pressure was increased by the rapid rate of change — teams of scientists on both sides of the Atlantic (including the science fiction writer Arthur C. Clarke) worked continuously to improve the state of the science. While the rapid advance of radar was a boon to the Allied forces, it created unique problems for electronics manufacturers, who struggled to keep up. Bemoaning production bottlenecks in 1944, one member of the War Production Board observed that "in the fast rising communication and electronics program, the [production] deficiency is in airborne radar in which design changes retard production."[23]

A can of KEMET getters, 1941.

Office Personnel
Typist-Clerk
Stenographer
Accountant-
Bookkeeper
**Lakewood
War Plant**
Air-Conditioned Office
Attractive Salaries
Permanent Position
**Kemet
Laboratories Co.,
Inc.**
Madison Ave. Opposite Newman
Telephone for Appointment
Ask for Mr. Hollingsworth
LA 4000—Extension 273.

Help wanted ad, Cleveland Plain Dealer, *1943.*

In his capacity as member of the War Production Board's committee on metallurgy, James Critchett was faced with the challenge of ensuring that the vital metals required for producing materials crucial to the war effort found their way to manufacturers in proper proportion. For example, barium and magnesium were vital to the production of vacuum tubes. But compounds of barium, especially barium nitrate, were also used for explosive devices, such as hand grenades, and magnesium was used in a great many metallurgical applications. The managers at KEMET had to work hard to obtain their raw materials.[23]

Wartime production presented other pressing needs as well, most notably for labor. During WWII, the organization, like many others, transformed virtually overnight. When the United States entered the war, American manufacturers across the board converted their facilities to aid the war effort. For some companies this meant retooling entirely; for others, it meant shifting production to accommodate military needs. KEMET's fortunes had grown with the rise of radio but in 1942 the marketplace was turned upside down. General Limitation Order No. L-44 froze production of radio sets to civilians. If that caused consternation at KEMET, the company need not have worried. As domestic sales ceased, military sales skyrocketed. From 1941 to 1943, monthly military radio sales jumped from $8 million to more than $200 million.[24]

KEMET responded by tripling its workforce. The company ran advertisements in the *Cleveland Plain Dealer* and other publications to find assembly workers and other plant personnel. Like so many other manufacturers, KEMET recruited women in record numbers to compensate for the dramatic shift in the labor force as men joined the armed forces. In 1939, KEMET employed 28 people in getters manufacturing, 29 percent of whom were women. By 1946, KEMET employed 83 people, 46 percent of whom were women. Many of these new employees, at KEMET as well as within other Union Carbide divisions in the National Carbon complex, were part of a large Slovakian community that had settled in the "Bird's Nest" area of Lakewood, OH. It was an explosion of production that left a lasting impact on KEMET.[26]

When the war ended in 1945, KEMET would sustain the momentum. Although military demands for getters slowed down, the research program in radar and other advanced electronics, including wartime technological advances, propelled new developments across the board.

Women workers kept KEMET's production lines moving during WWII.

Innovations like oscilloscopes, X-ray apparatus, and communication systems, kept government demand high for vacuum tubes outfitted with KEMET getters. One of the most important research programs centered on the computer. The Atanasoff-Berry computer (1943) and Colossus Mark 1 (1943) both relied on vacuum tubes for their operation. Between 1943 and 1945, the first generation of digital computing reached its peak with a machine called ENIAC (Electronic Numerical Integrator and Computer), which relied on a steady supply of vacuum tubes to operate. The ENIAC computer relied on 17,468 tubes, which had to be replaced at a rate of between one and five tubes every day. After the war, the first commercially produced digital computer was built in 1951 by Remington Rand — a company known for typewriters. Like ENIAC, the Remington Rand computer, called UNIVAC (Universal Automatic Computer), used 5,000 vacuum tubes to operate. KEMET components kept the machines running at peak efficiency.[27]

Although computer technology would drive the technological revolutions of the latter part of the century, it would be decades before they had any commercial possibility. KEMET's success in the postwar years would be driven by a new explosion in consumer electronics. The end of the war meant an end to civilian rationing, and the returning soldiers flush with success and steady paychecks created an economic boom. The civilian market for radios, virtually nonexistent in wartime, skyrocketed back to prewar levels, with 14 million sets produced in 1946. This rate would hold steady for the next 20 years. Plus there was a new product powered by vacuum tubes that would dramatically change the marketplace in consumer electronics: television.

Opposite: ENIAC (Electronic Numerical Integrator and Computer), the first programmable computer, depended on KEMET getters for efficient operation.

A 1947 magazine advertisement put KEMET getters in broader context.

As early as the 1920s, RCA and its affiliates had begun researching the possibilities of television. Major breakthroughs over the next decade allowed RCA to debut its first line of commercial televisions at the New York World's Fair in 1939. However, the United States was still in the grips of the Great Depression. In the late 1930s, the average per capita income was less than $700 ($12,500 in 2019 dollars). RCA's first television sets retailed at a cost between $395 and $675, making them far too expensive for anyone but a wealthy minority. During WWII, television technology was deemed inessential, and electronic manufacturers were directed to focus on radio and radar. Commercial development of television was placed on hold.[28]

continued on page 62

Visitors at the 1939 World's Fair gaze in wonder at a prototype television, housed in a cabinet of glass.

CATHODE RAY TUBES

Until the commercial development of flat panel displays in the late 1990s, television relied on cathode ray tubes (or CRTs). The CRT is a complex vacuum tube comprised of three elements: an electron "gun," a phosphorescent screen, and a glass envelope. The gun assembly projects a beam of electrons to the screen and contains an apparatus designed to manipulate the beam to produce an image. The entire apparatus is enclosed within a glass envelope consisting of a flat face plate (the screen), a funnel section, and a neck

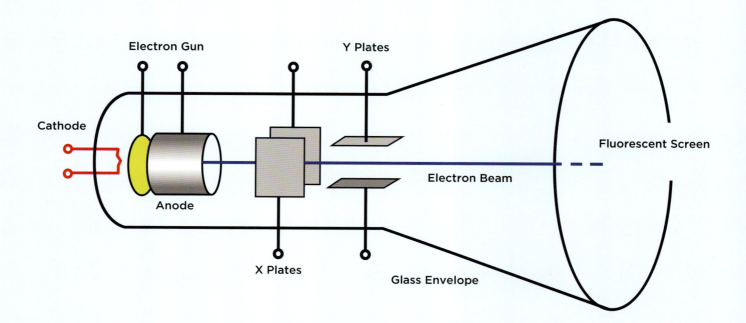

section. The neck houses the electron gun. The funnels houses coils and metal plates that focus and deflect the electron beam. The viewing surface on which the electrons are beamed is created through a thin layer of phosphor deposited on the inside of the face plate.

Color CRTs use three different phosphors, which emit red, green, and blue light respectively, and require three electron guns, one for each primary color. Although television screens and computer monitors are the best known use of CRTs, they were also commonly employed for oscilloscopes, radars, arcade videogames, specialized medical and industrial equipment, fluorescent displays, and other applications.

The development of the CRT is a prime example of international collaboration. Ferdinand Braun, a German physicist, produced the first CRT in 1897, drawing on theoretical discoveries made by German and British scientists in the preceding decades. John Bertrand Johnson, a Swedish immigrant, developed a CRT with a hot cathode in conjunction with his colleagues at Western Electric in 1922. Kenjiro Takayanagi, a Japanese engineer, built the world's first electronic television in 1925. Influenced by Takayanagi's work, Vladimir K. Zworykin, a Russian immigrant working for RCA, developed the first television system in 1932. The German firm Telefunken was the first to market televisions with CRTs in 1932. Interestingly, Mexican electrical engineer Guillermo González Camarena expanded upon this concept by patenting his "Chromoscopic Adapter for Television Equipment" 10 years later. This invention allowed for the transmission of color images, although it would be decades until the technology was widely adopted.

Like other tubes, the operation of CRTs depends upon the production of high vacuum, and relies on getters to absorb residual gases. Unlike radio tubes, CRTs also depend upon a uniform deposit of material on the interior of the tube to act as a screen. Because flashing a getter produces a deposit as gases combine with the getter material, special care is required to direct the flow of the residue to ensure that it does not interfere with the functioning of the screen. Produced in the form of an O, "ring getters" are mounted on top of an electron gun. A bent strip of metal known as a deflector aims the bright, silvery deposit towards the neck of the tube. Another style of getter mounts on an the anode contact and serves to deposit a thin film of barium over a large part of the internal surface of the tube, including the "shadow mask," a metal plate punched with minute holes that separate the colored phosphors on the screen. Non-evaporable getters — generally alloys of zirconium bonded to a metallic surface — remain in a solid state instead of being evaporated and condensed on a surface.

KEMET getters made early television possible. Until the division was sold to SAES Getters in 1987, KEMET produced almost all of the getters in the United States, and about 45 percent of the getters used worldwide. **K**

As soon as the war ended, RCA revived its program to produce televisions for commercial use. Technological developments during the war had raised the quality and lowered the cost of cathode ray tubes, screens, and other specialized components. As with radio, RCA owned most patents for television, but this time the company took a different approach. Rather than guarding its inventions, RCA shared them with its competitors. In 1946, the company's new CEO Frank M. Folsom invited other electronics manufacturers to examine its new television set and sent them home with blueprints for the product, encouraging them to produce their own. His plan was to flood the marketplace with television. For that to happen, no single company could maintain a stranglehold over the technology. But by sharing the blueprints, Folsom also ensured that other companies would follow the standards set by RCA, so no matter how many competitors were out there, RCA would remain its position of dominance. Folsom invested in television broadcasting, and developed a force of technicians to repair and maintain the new machines. As business historian Alfred D. Chandler remarked, "Folsom's strategy worked. U.S. television sales soared." In 1946, 6,000 homes in the United States had televisions; by 1955, fully *half* of all households in America had a set.[29]

The explosion of television created a boom for KEMET, which produced specialized getters for the new machines. In the mid 1950s, American manufacturers produced over 215 million receiving tubes and 10 million picture tubes. KEMET expanded its workforce accordingly. In just two years, from 1954 to 1956, the workforce at KEMET's Lakewood, OH, plant jumped from 167 people to 234, almost half of whom were women. KEMET would continue to be the largest American manufacturer of getters for television tubes until Union Carbide sold off that part of the business in 1987.[30]

KEMET's products sold for pennies, but they sold by the millions. With vacuum tubes in demand for televisions, audio equipment, and other applications, KEMET thrived. Getters were fundamental to the company's early success and growth, but with every technological innovation came new potential disruptions and opportunities. Even at the height of the vacuum tube, other advances were already emergent. In the 1950s, what began as an experimental program on the fringes of the getter division swiftly burgeoned into an altogether new product that would drive some of the greatest technological advances of the latter half of the twentieth century and beyond: the KEMET capacitor.

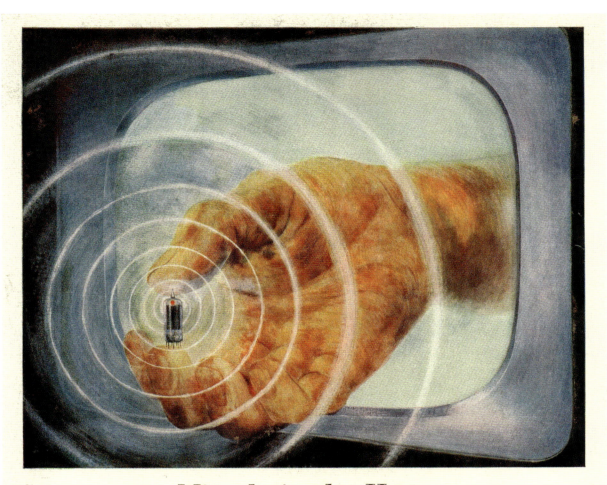

Miracle in the Home

The vacuum tube is working magic in our homes — to bring us the miracle of television

When the pianist strikes high "C" that string starts vibrating at more than 1,000 times per second—sending its musical tone across the room and perhaps across the nation.

But little tubes in your television set have electrical currents vibrating within them at more than 200 million times each second! That's almost beyond imagination.

FROM WAVES TO PICTURES—It's these tubes that make it possible for your set to receive the invisible television waves and convert them into the sound you hear and the picture you see.

One of the secrets of the tubes that perform such miracles is that they must operate under a high vacuum—as nearly nothing as possible.

HOW TO PRODUCE "NOTHING"—When the tube is being made, all possible air is pumped out and the tube is sealed. Then a tiny "getter"—built into the tube—is set off by electricity. There is a flash . . . and any remaining oxygen is burned up—leaving nothing.

UCC AND TELEVISION—Producing efficient getters for vacuum tubes is only one way in which the people of Union Carbide serve the electronics industry. They make ingredients for stainless steel that goes into picture tubes, chemicals for synthetic crystals, and plastics for insulation and for the cabinets themselves.

FREE: *Learn more about the interesting things you use every day. Write for the 1952 edition of the booklet "Products and Processes" which tells how science and industry use the ALLOYS, CARBONS, CHEMICALS, GASES, and PLASTICS made by Union Carbide. Ask for booklet D.*

UNION CARBIDE
AND CARBON CORPORATION
30 EAST 42ND STREET [UCC] NEW YORK 17, N. Y.

UCC's Trade-marked Products of Alloys, Carbons, Chemicals, Gases, and Plastics include

ELECTROMET Alloys and Metals • HAYNES STELLITE Alloys • NATIONAL Carbons • ACHESON Electrodes • PYROFAX Gas • EVEREADY Flashlights and Batteries
BAKELITE, KRENE, and VINYLITE Plastics • PREST-O-LITE Acetylene • LINDE Oxygen • PRESTONE and TREK Anti-Freezes • SYNTHETIC ORGANIC CHEMICALS

KEMET getters ushered in an age of wonder in this 1952 advertisement.

CHAPTER THREE:

DEVELOPING CAPACITY

The INVENTION OF THE TRANSISTOR IN 1947 UPENDED THE WORLD OF ELECTRONICS. Relying on the electronic properties of elemental materials, transistors represented the great breakthrough in solid-state physics. Like the vacuum tube, a transistor is a device used to amplify and regulate current. In contrast, however, the transistor conducts electricity through solid material, such as silicon or germanium, rather than through thermionic emission in a vacuum. Smaller, lighter, cheaper, and more efficient than vacuum tubes, transistors changed the rules of the game. They allowed for the development of more easily portable variations of established products — the transistor radio, introduced in 1954, is a case in point. More significantly, they opened the field for the development of new complex electronics, and a new industry structured on the unique powers of the semiconductor. The transistor would make possible the exploration of space and the invention of the Internet. More immediately, it launched a race among companies keen to explore the potentials of solid-state electronics. The wave of innovation launched by the solid-state revolution would sweep KEMET in an entirely new direction, and give rise to the company's signature product: the tantalum capacitor.

The early history of the transistor demonstrated the benefits of taking advantage of the latest innovations. John Bardeen and Walter Brattain, two physicists at Bell Labs, invented the first "point-contact" transistor in December 1947. Their colleague William Shockley improved the invention in January 1948 with the "junction" transistor, which became the model for later manufactures after Bell announced the discovery in July 1951. But it was a small upstart company, Texas Instruments (TI), that reaped the benefits. The transistors that Bell invented — and licensed — were made of germanium, which had certain limitations. At TI, a scientific team led by Gordon Teal, who had worked at Bell Labs before moving back to his native

The first commercial silicon transistor transformed Texas Instruments into an industry leader.

Texas, developed the first commercial silicon transistors. Between 1954 and 1960, TI's income from transistor sales leaped from several hundred thousand dollars a year to over $80 million ($678 million in 2019 dollars) a year. TI's product became the new industry standard, and a relatively marginal firm had become a major player.[1]

KEMET personnel at other divisions of Union Carbide saw the runaway success of TI and recognized the future of electronics. To stay current, the company would have to join the revolution. But there was one problem: no division at Union Carbide was equipped for research in solid-state physics.

Research and development were the heart and soul of Union Carbide, and the corporation had multiple labs across its many divisions. These labs were devoted to chemicals, plastics, industrial gases, metals, and carbon products such as batteries. But the corporation's subsidiaries did not focus on the new science. Thus the corporation, which usually was swift to find ways of staying near the cutting edge, was very slow to capitalize on the invention of the transistor. In 1952, the first year that transistors were introduced to the general market, there were five companies manufacturing the component. By 1955, there were 26. Union Carbide did not offer anything in the way of transistors until 1965.[2]

1947
Scientists at Bell Labs invent the transistor, inaugurating a new age in electronics.

1958
KEMET introduces its first line of capacitors.

1962
KEMET supplies capacitors for Telstar, the world's first active communications satellite, and becomes a major supplier for the space and defense industries.

1963
Responding to burgeoning demand, KEMET opens a production plant in Simpsonville, SC.

1971
KEMET closes capacitor production in Cleveland, OH, to relocate its major operations in South Carolina.

1980s
KEMET invests tens of millions of dollars to develop facilities for manufacturing surface-mount devices (SMDs) to supply growing demands.

1984
An environmental disaster in Bhopal, India, initiates the downfall of Union Carbide, KEMET's parent company.

1950-1954
Scientists at Bell Labs and Sprague invent the tantalum capacitor.

1959
David E. Maguire joins Union Carbide as a production engineer in Fremont, OH.

1969
KEMET introduces its first multilayer ceramic capacitor; KEMET opens its first international plant, in Matamoros, Mexico.

1977
Apple, RadioShack, and Commodore inaugurate a new industry with the first widely available personal computers.

SOLID-STATE PHYSICS AND THE TRANSISTOR

The transistor and the tantalum capacitor were the tangible products of research that had been ongoing in the field of solid-state physics since the 1930s.

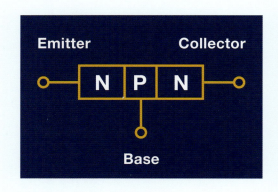

A n-p-n transistor uses the natural properties of solid materials to amplify current.

Solid-state physics serves as one of the core theoretical bases of the science of materials. It draws from the fundamental insight that many solid materials are composed of atoms packed tightly together in a regular geometrical pattern — a crystal lattice. Atoms are themselves composed of electrons orbiting a nucleus. In metals, electrons are shared throughout the crystalline structure through a process known as covalent bonding. This structure gives crystalline solids basic properties relating to the conduction of heat and electricity. But those properties are different depending on the materials, and can be manipulated through the introduction of impurities, a process known as "doping."

Metals are examples of conductors — heat one end of a metal bar, and the other end becomes hot very quickly. Wood and plastics, on the other hand, have a very different atomic structure, and do not conduct heat or electricity; they are known as insulators. Semiconductors such as silicon and germanium are materials whose conductivity is lower than metals by many orders of magnitude. "Doping" semiconductors affects their behavior in dramatic ways. Adding some elements (such as arsenic or phosphorus) to silicon creates a surplus of electrons; the electrons flow out of it. Adding other elements (such as boron or aluminum) will make electrons from nearby materials flow into it. These two forms of silicon are known as n-type (negative) and p-type (positive) silicon.

A transistor is created by layering n-type and p-type silicon into a "sandwich." Attaching electrical contacts to each layer of the sandwich produces means of amplifying current, directing its flow, and switching it on and off. In a simple n-p-n sandwich, for example, electrons flow from the n-type into the p-type, where they accumulate until they are pulled out by another layer of n-type. The effect creates a large output from a small input. **K**

Union Carbide's new state-of-the-art laboratory in Parma, OH, helped KEMET to develop its tantalum capacitor.

Recognizing that they were arriving late to the game, Union Carbide established a new research program in 1955. The company built a state-of-the-art facility in Parma, OH, under the supervision of the National Carbon division to serve as a center for bringing Union Carbide into the new era, with 175,000 square feet of floor space and 350 new personnel.[3] For their first director, they hired Robert G. Breckenridge (1916-1986), who had taught solid-state physics at MIT after receiving his Ph.D. The Parma lab was located only six miles from the National Carbon complex in Lakewood, OH, that housed the carbon products division and KEMET, so communication between the two facilities was continuous. It was too late for Union Carbide to pursue transistors, but it was just the right moment to take advantage of another advance in solid state electronics — the tantalum capacitor.

The solid-state capacitor was another invention of Bell Labs. In 1950, Horace E. Haring and Raymond L. Taylor designed a capacitor featuring an anode made of tantalum powder that had been rolled into a cylinder and sintered into a pellet surrounded by a wet electrolyte acting as the cathode.[4] Independently, Preston Robinson, director of research at Sprague Electric, which was then the world's largest manufacturer of electronic components, was exploring the same materials. Robinson had attended MIT and the

Preston Robinson, a scientist at Sprague Electric, invented the tantalum capacitor in 1954.

University of California before joining Sprague Electric in 1929. He was by far the company's most prolific scientist. He beat Bell Labs to the punch with his patent for a tantalum capacitor, filed in 1954.[5] It was his 101st invention, and it proved to be his most lucrative. With process modifications introduced by his colleague, Richard J. Millard at Sprague Electric, Robinson's design would serve at the fundamental basis for all commercially produced tantalum capacitors for decades.[6]

Although Robinson was awarded the patent, this was only after a long legal struggle. Shortly after Robinson had filed his application, Bell Labs initiated a patent suit claiming priority for Haring and Taylor's invention. The U.S. Board of Patent Interferences ultimately found in favor of Sprague in a case that would last almost 10 years. By then, the component was being used widely in military, industrial, and commercial applications, as well as specialized miniature applications like hearing aids. Sales of tantalum capacitors in 1964 exceeded $29 million per year (about $235 million in 2019 dollars).[7]

The nearly 10 year lawsuit between Bell Labs and Sprague Electric offered an opportunity for companies like Union Carbide, who recognized that in such circumstances it was easier to ask for forgiveness than permission. Companies had a rare opportunity to establish a market for their products before paying licensing fees. Guided by solid-state scientists at Parma, OH, KEMET had begun commercial production of tantalum capacitors as quickly as possible, starting production in 1957 and introducing their first line in early 1959.[8] Once Sprague Electrics' lawsuit with Bell Labs was finally settled, Union Carbide paid the company a "substantial sum" for past production, and future licensing.[9]

KEMET's scientific team in the late 1950s and early 1960s was led by Johann Siegfried Wagener. Born in 1908, Siegfried Wagener had attended the University of Berlin and was the author of a number of works on thermionics including a two volume work on oxide coated cathodes. He also wrote science fiction on the side. After a postwar stint in London, Wagener moved to Cleveland to accept the post of research director at KEMET.[10] The scientist who most closely supervised KEMET's work on tantalum capacitors was Howard S. Pattin. A much beloved figure who afforded

THE TANTALUM CAPACITOR

A capacitor is a passive electronic component that stores and releases energy. In its most basic construction, a capacitor consists of two electrical conductors (plates) separated by an insulating (dielectric) medium. When placed in a circuit, an electric charge builds up, causing one plate to gain a positive charge, and the other a negative charge. The capacitor stores the charge until it has built up to a certain level, at which point the current is released across the dielectric and into the system. Unlike a battery, which stores energy and releases it slowly, capacitors generally release energy in bursts, though these bursts might be microseconds apart. They are used to smooth the voltage in circuits, and control the release of energy. They are used to filter certain signals, and serve as timing devices and tuners.

Above: Some of the different tantalum capacitors KEMET has made over the years.
Left: A microscopic view of the sintered tantalum inside a capacitor.

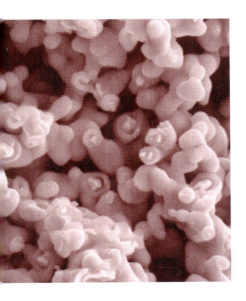

The capacitance — or the amount of energy a capacitor can store — is subject to multiple variables, including the area of the plates, the distance between them, and the materials used as an insulator. Dielectrics may be made of glass, paper, plastic, mica, ceramic, metal oxides, or other materials. Some capacitors — those used in transistor radios — rely on air to separate the plates. Because the operation of a capacitor is a function of its structure, they can detect tiny changes. For this reason they are very effective as sensors to detect changes in acceleration, pressure, humidity, fuel levels, and other mechanical functions. In computers, capacitors produce the rapid bursts of charge that convey binary data.

Tantalum, whose dielectric properties had been studied since the 1930s, has very high capacitance in contrast with other materials, and is very lightweight. The first "wet" tantalum capacitors used an electrolyte of acid or a paste of strong salts. These are still used in some applications. The new design that revolutionized the field was a solid construction, and this made it unusually stable, shock resistant, and impervious to changes in temperature — perfect for space exploration, where materials had to withstand both extreme heat and extreme cold. Tantalum powder pressed and sintered into the pellet that serves as the anode at the core of the capacitor is highly porous, a quality that vastly increases the surface area, and therefore the capacitance of the component. **K**

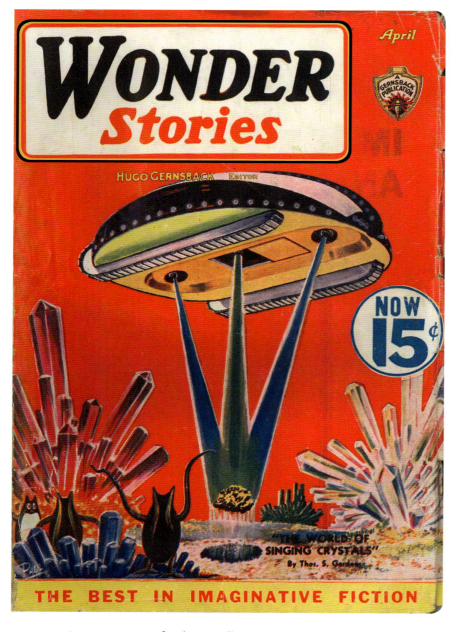

A science fiction pulp with a story by Siegfried Wagener, KEMET's director of research during the transition to capacitors.

a striking contrast to the stern and straight backed Wagener, Pattin joined Union Carbide in 1937 shortly after completing his Ph.D. at the University of Illinois at Urbana-Champaign. Pattin's initial work was with ultraviolet spectroscopy and X-ray diffraction, but during WWII he shifted to electrochemistry. Like Nobelist Linus Pauling, computer pioneer Jacob Rabinow, and Telstar Project Director Alton C. Dickieson, Pattin was awarded a Naval Ordnance Development Award in 1945 for work on the proximity fuze — a project led by Sprague Electrics' Preston Robinson.[11] At KEMET, "Doc" Pattin received patents for getter assemblies and oversaw the high reliability (hi-rel) division, developing processes for failure analysis. (See the sidebar on page 72.)

KEMET enjoyed three distinct advantages at the outset, all devolving from its status as a branch of a large, diverse company. First was the financial and logistical support of the corporation in general and the Parma research center in particular, where researchers worked alongside scientists at KEMET to develop new products. Second was a ready supply of tantalum, which beginning in 1962 was produced in house by another division of Union Carbide, the Haynes Stellite Company.[12] The third, and doubtless most important factor that paved the way for KEMET's early success, was the fact that Union Carbide already had a long established business relationship with the biggest customers for capacitors, including the United States government. Union Carbide was one of the major suppliers of military equipment during WWI, providing everything from helium for dirigibles, ferrozirconium for armor plating, and activated carbon for gas masks. During WWII, the company supplied the U.S. Armed Forces with butane, polyethylene, synthetic gem bearings — and getters. Union Carbide developed sapphire windows for the Navy's Sidewinder missiles during the Korean War, and produced great quantities of liquid oxygen, nitrogen, and hydrogen for the Space Race.[13] Union Carbide's connections helped KEMET's top of the line capacitors garner attention as soon as the new product was introduced to the market.

Even so, success was not immediate. In addition to tantalum capacitors, KEMET experimented with a range of other new products to supplement its getters division. These included pure silicon for transistors, and silicon monoxide, used as a protective coating for high quality lenses, fuel cells, and thin film components. Managerial upheaval contributed to the problem. In 1959, KEMET's president John D. McQuade retired after almost 30 years of service. Rather than replace him with a new president, Union Carbide installed a general manager who by all reports was highly competent but had no experience with electronic components. The general manager reported to Union Carbide executives who were based in New York, NY, and Indianapolis, IN, both far from Cleveland. Effectively orphaned, KEMET existed in a sort of limbo for several years before 1962, when it was consolidated under the Linde division, which produced industrial gases and synthetic crystals. During these years, the company's survival was far from certain. Wayne Hazen, who joined KEMET in 1961, had heard about a visit from a manager from Union Carbide that happened just before was hired. "He'd come in there to shut the place down. And he looked at the whole operation, and he said, "'No, we're not going to shut it down. Let's just build it up.'"[14]

SOLID TANTALUM CAPACITORS

● NEW IN THIS EDITION . . . Specifications for insulating sleeves, page 2. Minor revisions in some capacitor sizes, page 3.

KEMET solid tantalum capacitors are designed to meet industry's growing need for capacitors which are small physically, large electrically, and very reliable, even in environments which are dynamically and thermally severe.

The excellence of tantalum and of its dielectric oxide as capacitor materials is widely known.

High capacity per unit volume, low dissipation, long shelf life and stability of capacitors made from these materials, have established them in critical electronic circuitry. Now their usefulness is extended to wider temperature ranges, longer shelf lives and more rigorous dynamic loads through Kemet Company's solid construction.

KEMET capacitors contain no liquid electrolyte. They are hermetically sealed, do not need to breathe, and have nothing to leak. Shelf life, whether measured in terms of capacitance change or increase of leakage current, is much longer than with previous electrolytic capacitors, even tantalum.

The requirements of MIL-C-3965B are met by these capacitors for all three grades of vibration. They have, in fact, been subjected to 40 g's from 10 to 2000 cycles without measurable electrical changes.

Kemet Company is not dependent upon other suppliers for the mining or processing of tantalum. It is therefore possible to firmly control each step in capacitor manufacture, from raw materials to the finished product, to obtain the utmost in quality and reliability.

Performance characteristics, typical performance curves and tabulated specifications are presented in the pages that follow.

APPLICATIONS...

A FEW of the many applications for which KEMET solid tantalum capacitors are ideally suited are mentioned here.

TRANSISTOR AMPLIFIERS . . . Where low circuit impedance demands high capacitance, low leakage and small size. Use for coupling, by-pass, filter and similar applications.

R-C TIMING CIRCUITS . . . Excellent temperature stability and low leakage current make KEMET solid tantalum capacitors suitable for critical time delay circuits—even under severe temperature and vibration conditions.

ANALOG COMPUTERS . . . For performing such operations as differentiating and integrating with high reliability in minimum space.

TRIGGERING CIRCUITS . . . Where stored energy must be available under adverse environments after long periods of inactivity.

POWER SUPPLIES . . . In low voltage filter circuits demanding high capacitance and low leakage current where reliability over wide temperature ranges and severe mechanical stresses is required — and space is at a premium.

KEMET introduced its first line of capacitors in late 1958.

What changed Union Carbide's mind was that KEMET had suddenly become profitable. Between 1960 and 1961, sales of tantalum capacitors jumped 89 percent. "Tantalum capacitors are now the division's chief product," was the definitive declaration in the corporation's annual report.[15] Boeing had discovered KEMET, as had other airplane manufacturers in the United States and England. KEMET products were used in the British Aircraft Corporation's VC 10 and the Minuteman Intercontinental Ballistic Missile. Most prestigiously, KEMET was selected to provide capacitors for Telstar, the world's first active communications satellite. Built by Bell Labs and launched by NASA on July 10, 1962, Telstar had a diameter of less than 1 meter and weighed just 80 kilograms. Every component counted. Parts needed to be not only light and compact, but also durable enough to withstand the rigors of space travel, and because replacing them in space would be impossible, they had to be built to last forever. Telstar required 36 different types of capacitors, 380 in all, and each was rigorously examined and tested over a range of environmental conditions.

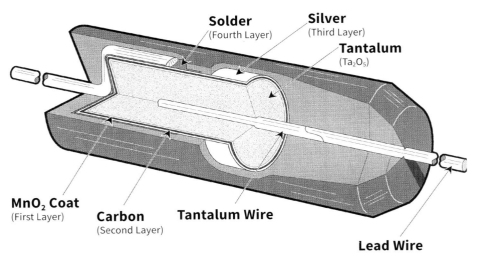

KEMET® Electronics Corporation
Typical Axial Molded Solid Tantalum Capacitor

Solder
(Fourth Layer)

Silver
(Third Layer)

Tantalum
(Ta₂O₅)

MnO₂ Coat
(First Layer)

Carbon
(Second Layer)

Tantalum Wire

Lead Wire

©1990 KEMET Electronics Corporation

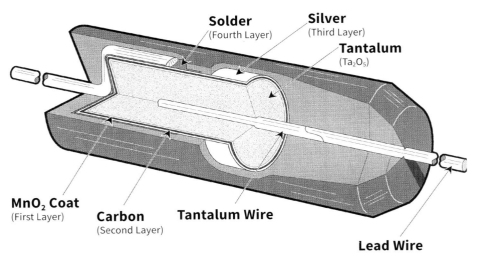

Axial capacitors with a solid tantalum core were KEMET's major product from 1958 to the mid 1980s, when sales of surface mount devices (see p. 80 and p. 94) began to gain popularity. KEMET still produces capacitors based on this classic design.

The publicity generated by Telstar, along with a rush of orders for other projects, catapulted KEMET's capacitor business from its uncertain beginnings. Union Carbide president Birney Mason, Jr., announced his intention "to broaden and to define more clearly the Corporation's future role in electronics."[16] Mason put his money where his mouth was. In 1962, KEMET doubled its capacitor production plant at the National Carbon complex in Cleveland. That made for cramped conditions in a plant that already housed a number of production facilities and laboratories.

KEMET getters were assembled and packed at one end of the building, and the capacitor unit was scattered throughout. At one station engineers pressed tantalum powder into pellets fitted around a tantalum wire, and baked them at a high temperature to create a sintered solid that served as the anode core. At another station the pellet was submerged in a bath of a weak acid solution that created through electrolysis an oxide layer that would serve as the dielectric. Then the pellet was dipped into a manganese nitrate solution (a process known as impregnation), which formed a layer of manganese dioxide when heated; this served as the cathode. Yet another station dipped the pellet into silver to provide a good connection for the cathode. Finally, there was assembly: a cathode wire was welded on, and everything was placed within a "can" — a metal case — that was filled with solder to create an electrical connection to the can. And then there was quality control and testing. Every step of the process required careful measurement and control which had to be adjusted to accommodate different sizes and product lines. The process then was very much like it is today with one major difference: it was all done by hand. One visitor to the Cleveland plant compared what he saw to "giving birth to a porcupine."[17]

continued on page 76

Opposite: Engineers at Bell Labs at work on Telstar, 1962. The world's first active communications satellite depended on 36 types of KEMET capacitors, 380 in all. It was KEMET's first major project.

HI-REL CAPACITORS AND FAILURE ANALYSIS

From the beginning, KEMET has offered capacitors in two varieties: commercial and high reliability "hi-rel." The two varieties are identical, except that hi-rel capacitors are subjected to a vigorous regimen of tests. Following a broad approach developed by chemist Henry Eyring, components are placed in "accelerated" conditions, and subjected to much higher voltages and more extreme temperatures than they would normally encounter. Noting the rate at which capacitors fail under such stressful conditions allows one to calculate their life expectancy under anticipated uses. The equations for making such calculations were developed by the Swedish statistician Waloddi Weibull, whose works on fatigue analysis became the mathematical gold standard for determining reliability.

Typically, one takes a batch of capacitors, places a portion of them under test conditions, and notes the distribution of failures over time: one might fail immediately, another might fail at two hours, a third at 100 hours, a fourth at 10,000 hours. From these statistics one is able to grade the batch to a particular failure rate level. Alternatively, one might

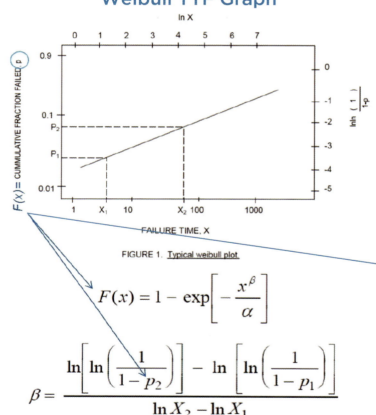

Weibull TTF Graph

FIGURE 1. Typical weibull plot

$$F(x) = 1 - \exp\left[-\frac{x^\beta}{\alpha}\right]$$

$$\beta = \frac{\ln\left[\ln\left(\dfrac{1}{1-p_2}\right)\right] - \ln\left[\ln\left(\dfrac{1}{1-p_1}\right)\right]}{\ln X_2 - \ln X_1}$$

separately test each capacitor designated for an exceptional application. This is what KEMET has typically done for important space projects such as Telstar, the Apollo missions, and the Mir Space Station.

Unlike batteries and light bulbs, that generally show a decline in efficacy until they wear out, tantalum capacitors continue to perform. The longer they are used, the better they work. Hi-rel capacitors can last for decades. Capacitor manufacturers measure the "failure in time" (FIT) rate in terms of the number of failures per billion hours of use. Hi-rel capacitors are especially important for defense and aerospace applications where components are expected to last indefinitely. They are also important for certain medical applications such as pacemakers, where reliability is literally a matter of life or death.[18]

Because testing is a slow and complex process, and screening protocols are often customized according to specific customer requirements, hi-rel components can be up to twenty times more expensive than commercial components. **K**

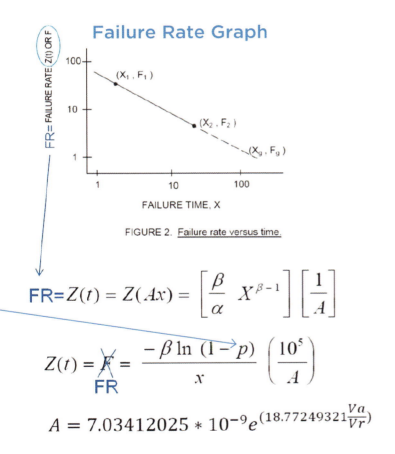

FIGURE 2. Failure rate versus time.

$$FR = Z(t) = Z(Ax) = \left[\frac{\beta}{\alpha} X^{\beta-1} \right] \left[\frac{1}{A} \right]$$

$$Z(t) = F = \frac{-\beta \ln (1-p)}{x} \left(\frac{10^5}{A} \right)$$

$$A = 7.03412025 * 10^{-9} e^{\left(18.77249321 \frac{Va}{Vr} \right)}$$

KEMET uses models by the statistician Waloddi Weibull to grade capacitor reliability.

Production started out slowly but by the early 1960s the company was producing half a million capacitors per week, with no signs of slowing down. Sprague Electric and KEMET were friendly rivals, with the two vying for the top spot as America's number one producer of tantalum capacitors. They used identical processes (KEMET had licensed the patents from Sprague), offered parallel product lines, and maintained equivalent standards of quality. So the two companies helped each other out. If KEMET had too large an order to fill on time, the managers would order some unlabeled components from Sprague; likewise, when Sprague fell short KEMET would send over a batch printed with Sprague numbers.

In 1962, Union Carbide increased KEMET operations in Ohio by 50 percent. The corporation's major facility in England began capacitor production to reach the European market. C. Robert Castor,

Union Carbide's Aycliffe plant began producing KEMET capacitors. Note that Linde products (laser crystals) here are offered under the KEMET name.

KEMET's plant in Simpsonville, SC, was intended to serve only as a manufacturing facility but soon became the company's headquarters.

then serving as general manager of KEMET, started searching for a location to build a new, dedicated manufacturing plant. Besides wanting to expand, there was another good reason to shift KEMET operations away from the National Carbon Building. "Carbon impurity in a tantalum anode is a disaster," explains Dale Hazen, who joined KEMET after he graduated college in 1961. "All you had to have was somebody shake the rafters of that building and ..."[19] Castor would find the perfect spot in an underdeveloped tract ten miles south of Greenville, SC. Ground was broken in 1963, and by the end of the year there was a new 40,000 square foot facility on a 40-acre lot in Simpsonville, SC, with plenty of room for expansion.

The move split the company. Dale Hazen, who worked in commercial products, shifted to Simpsonville in 1964. His cousin Wayne Hazen, who worked in hi-rel, stayed behind. Wagener, the director of research, took the opportunity to return to Europe. As the facility in South Carolina grew, it became increasingly apparent that consolidation would be beneficial. Finally in 1971, KEMET closed its capacitor operations at the National Carbon plant in Lakewood, OH. KEMET's getters division, holding steady at the top of the market in North America, stayed behind. About 10 percent of the 400 people working on capacitors moved to the area around Simpsonville, SC. The rest transferred to other divisions within Union Carbide. The shift created a cadre of expatriates who had worked together in Ohio; they were known locally as the Cleveland Mafia. Among the Mafiosi was a young engineer who had been rising steadily through the ranks since his arrival at KEMET in 1961, Dave Maguire (1934-2007). Appointed general manager in 1973, he would lead the company through its remaining years at Union Carbide, and serve as president and CEO when KEMET was established as an independent company in 1987.

A keychain with a golden capacitor at the center was given to employees in 1973 to celebrate the company's tenth anniversary in South Carolina.

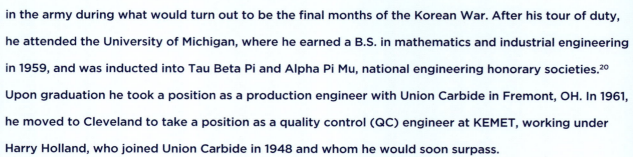

DAVID E. MAGUIRE

The man who would lead KEMET through its growth into an independent company demonstrated himself early on to be a man of promise. Born in Grosse Pointe, MI, in 1934, David Maguire enlisted in the army during what would turn out to be the final months of the Korean War. After his tour of duty, he attended the University of Michigan, where he earned a B.S. in mathematics and industrial engineering in 1959, and was inducted into Tau Beta Pi and Alpha Pi Mu, national engineering honorary societies.[20] Upon graduation he took a position as a production engineer with Union Carbide in Fremont, OH. In 1961, he moved to Cleveland to take a position as a quality control (QC) engineer at KEMET, working under Harry Holland, who joined Union Carbide in 1948 and whom he would soon surpass.

DAVID E. MAGUIRE

Maguire Moves From Carbide To Kemet Unit

A. J. Adams, vice president of Union Carbide Consumer Products company, has announced that effective February 15, David E. Maguire, a production engineer with the Fremont plant for the past two years, will be transferred to the Kemet company, Cleveland. The Kemet company is the electronics division of Union Carbide specializing in barium getters for vacuum tubes, ultra pure silicon for transistors, and tantalum capacitors.

Maguire is the son of Dr. and Mrs. Clarence E. Maguire, Grosse Pointe, Mich. He attended the Massachusetts Institute of Technology and was graduated from the University of Michigan in 1959 with degrees in Industrial Engineering and Mathematics. He is a member of Tau Beta Pi and Alpha Pi Mu, national engineering honorary societies. Before attending college, Maguire served with the army for three years which included a European tour of duty.

He is a member of the Fremont Rifle and Pistol Club and is a life member of the National Rifle Association. Also included in his interests are advanced electronics with emphasis on controls for automation.

Maguire, his wife, the former Madalyn Jones of Fremont, and their baby daughter, Dawn, will be moving to Cleveland as soon as housing arrangements can be completed.

Described by everyone who knew him as an intensely driven man with a keen eye for detail, a terrifyingly precise memory, and a fierce devotion to his company — in later years he was at his desk six and a half days a week, working from 8:00 A.M. to 5:00 P. M. — Maguire swiftly established himself as a leader. After his first year, he was promoted to quality control supervisor, then manager of hi-rel production, then quality assurance manager. It was Maguire who developed the system of grading capacitors by failure rate according to Weibull distribution scores. During evenings and weekends he worked on an independent project, inventing a machine that would measure the capacitance and dissipation factor of a capacitor.[21] Assembling the devices in his basement and marketing them under the name of the D. M. Research Corporation, he sold them to KEMET and other capacitor manufacturers. Reportedly, when Union Carbide learned that Maguire was the figure behind D. M. Research, they promoted him yet again.

Maguire transitioned to Simpsonville, SC, between 1966 and 1967, assuming the post of manager of technology. In 1972 he was made general manager of KEMET and in 1978, vice president of Union Carbide's Consumer Electronics division. Generally avoiding the limelight — his one public appearance outside of KEMET was at a conference to present a technical paper on hybrid circuits[22] — he was universally acknowledged as the heart and soul of the company, ushering it forward and pulling it through difficult times through sheer force of will. **K**

When he announced that KEMET was building a new facility in Simpsonville, SC, Castor emphasized that the talents of the people of South Carolina served as one of the draws. Greenville Technical College had recently been established, and there was ample talent in the area. "Ours is a high reliability product, but [it is] no better than the people who make it," Castor said.[23] The company drew from a wide population, including a large pool of women workers, who by most accounts made up over 80 percent of the manufacturing force. In 1974, the company was the largest employer of women in Greenville County.[24] It was widely believed in the 1960s that women were particularly well suited for assembly work that required manual dexterity. But women soon found themselves doing work that broke the usual gender barriers. "I was the truck driver that drove back from building to building, loading stuff for a while," laughed Bonnie Craven, who started in 1969 and retired after 40 years. "I never dreamed I could drive a truck, but I did."[25]

South Carolinians were attracted to jobs at the new plant for all sorts of reasons. Union Carbide offered higher pay and better benefits than the textile mills that comprised Greenvlle's major industry. The fact that the new factory had air conditioning was another plus; in the early 1960s, that was still a novelty among industries in the South. Bill Stone, the first human resources manager at KEMET's Simpsonville plant, was from the area and did much to recruit workers and build a sense of community. The workplace ethos he established was continued by his successors; most people speak of KEMET in South Carolina as being like an extended family.

KEMET's plant in South Carolina was the largest employer of women in the county.

Jeanette Simpson was a young mother when she joined KEMET in the summer of 1966. Her husband traveled for work, and her youngest child was in the third grade. "I was sitting there with nothing to do all day." And she wanted a new bedroom set. After a series of medical tests she was assigned to a bench welding J-series capacitors during third shift, which ran from midnight to 8:00 A.M. She had not intended it as a permanent job, but she stayed at KEMET for 30 years, working primarily as a process inspector.[26]

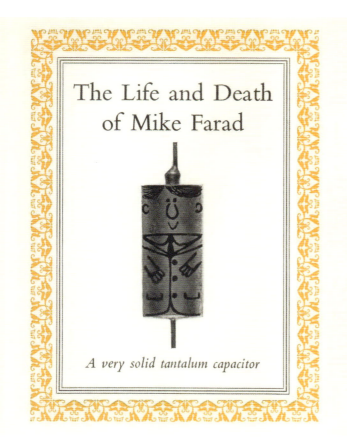

The Life and Death of Mike Farad

A very solid tantalum capacitor

A whimsical booklet produced in the early 1960s to promote KEMET products plays on the term microfarad (μF), a unit of capacitance.

KEMET offered a boon for many young men too. Dick Thompson joined Union Carbide in 1966 right after his graduation from Iowa State University. A week later he was summoned to the local draft board for a physical, as the Vietnam War was heating up. He returned to work expecting to be called to duty, but was surprised to receive a letter of deferment. KEMET had a number of military contracts, so the board determined that the best way for Thompson to serve his country was to continue his work in the lab.[27]

Relocating operations to South Carolina allowed the company to diversify its offerings, and KEMET grew rapidly. In 1967, KEMET introduced its first line of ceramic capacitors, a move that would almost double its income. By the 1980s, KEMET would be the second largest manufacturer of ceramic capacitors in the world. In addition to surface-mounted "chips", KEMET produced the "Blue Max," a subminiature, precision, epoxy-dipped, radial-leaded, monolithic, ceramic capacitor. New tantalum offerings included the T390/T392 series of capacitors coated in epoxy. Economical and compact, these "dipped" products were designed to accommodate increasingly compact applications. In 1973, the company shipped 540 million tantalum capacitors valued at $115 million (about $650 million in 2019 dollars), and 490 million ceramic pieces, valued at $95 million (over $535 million in 2019 dollars).[28]

A KEMET ad celebrating its highly successful work on the Viking mission to Mars.

The postwar boom in electronics fueled KEMET's rapid growth in the 1960s. The company became known as a supplier of high performance capacitors for the defense industry and was a major contributor to the U.S. space race, tailoring components for major missions to the Moon, Mars, and beyond. These were high stakes assignments. For example, the Viking mission to Mars involved two space probes — one orbiting the planet, the other exploring the surface — that were launched in 1975. The gap between the production of the parts and the launch of spacecraft was two years. The son of one KEMET engineer remembered his father's anxiety. The boy was getting ready for school and saw his father, who normally left early, in the living room watching TV. What was going on? "Those are my capacitors," his father said, pointing to the launch being televised, "and if they don't start, I don't need to go into work today."[29]

continued on page 84

CERAMIC CHIPS

Different varieties of ceramic have been used as dielectrics in capacitors since the 1920s. The range of available material allows for the production of a variety of capacitors with different characteristics. The original design of ceramic capacitors was simple: two electrodes separated by a ceramic disk, dipped in a protective coating. KEMET's Blue Max is an example of this construction.

The real breakthrough came with the development of the surface-mounted ceramic chip in the 1960s. These consist of alternating layers of electrode and dielectic, producing high capacitance in a small, efficient package. Depending on the desired effect, there may be hundreds or even thousands of layers, and the layers may be ultra thin to create miniature products. The smallest ceramic chip KEMET produces is 0.25 x 0.13 mm, smaller than a grain of salt.

The manufacturing process is very complex. First comes the preparation of the dielectric. Ceramic powders are mixed in a slurry. After undergoing several processes for purification, the material is coated on a carrier film, which is then dried to produce thin sheets of ceramic tape. Next comes the preparation of the electrodes, which were originally made from palladium, but today are more commonly made from nickel.

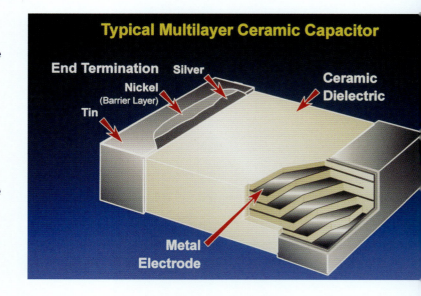

Typical Multilayer Ceramic Capacitor

End Termination
Silver
Nickel (Barrier Layer)
Tin
Ceramic Dielectric
Metal Electrode

The ceramic sheets are coated with a layer of electrodes arranged in a pattern. Today the electrodes are printed with a screen printer that is the industrial analogue to the device used for printing t-shirts. But in the beginning, they were arranged by hand and the ceramic tape had to be carefully fitted to the electrode layer. Multiple ceramic/electrode layers and tape are stacked in an alternating structure to make a pad. The pad is then cut to produce the individual chips, which are baked and fired. The corners of each chip are rounded to prevent damage, rinsed, and dried. The ends are trimmed and the chips are dipped in a metal paste to form external electrodes. The chip is fired once more, then electroplated first with nickel then with tin. Each chip is then tested for capacitance and dissipation factor before being packaged and shipped. Everything is done in a "clean room," where personnel wear surgical scrubs, hair caps, and gloves to ensure that each batch remains free of impurities. **K**

Above: Before automation, ceramic capacitors were made by hand.

Left: A modern plant for manufacturing KEMET ceramic capacitors.

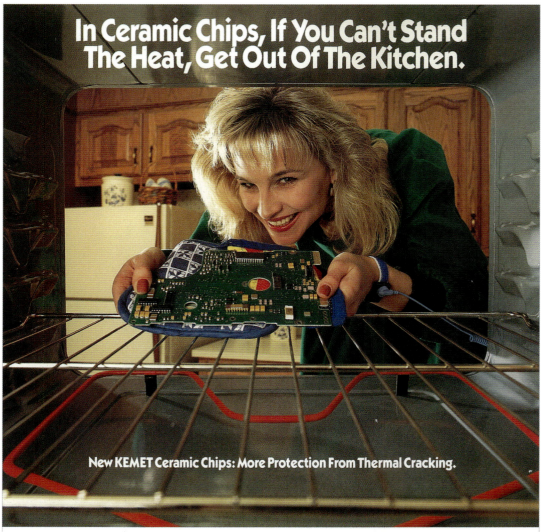

KEMET ad from 1989 redefines what it means to bake chips.

Closer to earth, KEMET also supplied parts for the rapidly growing field of automotive electronics. In 1955, Chrysler and Philco teamed up to develop a tubeless radio, the Mopar Model 914HR. In 1963, Pontiac offered an automatic ignition system, the Delcotronic. Antilock brakes were invented in 1971, electronic control modules for internal combustion engines in 1979, and airbags in

1988. KEMET developed specialized capacitors to facilitate these developments every step of the way. Ford Motor Company was one of KEMET's biggest customers, and one of its most satisfied, presenting the company with many of its annual vendor awards recognizing consistent quality.

By the 1970s, the burgeoning computer industry offered another major area of growth. It was also a space in which KEMET had operated for years. Univac, which developed the first commercial computer in 1951, was an early customer of KEMET, as was Hewlett-Packard. After the invention of the microprocessor in 1968, computing power expanded exponentially, and in 1977, Apple, Commodore, and RadioShack introduced the first personal computers to the wider market. Leaded capacitors needed to have their wires fitted through holes in a circuit board, but KEMET's ceramic chips were suited to mount directly. This saved both time and space, facilitating miniaturization.

By 1968, KEMET had 1,000 employees in Simpsonville, SC. The closure of the company's operations in Cleveland in 1971 — precipitated by a dip in the capacitor market in 1970 — meant a new building and 275 new hires in Simpsonville. By 1974, the company's workforce numbered approximately 2,225 people, and its facilities had expanded from 40,000 to about 275,000 square feet. As the company grew, engineers at the company began to develop equipment to automate the processes. Dave Steigerwald, a native of Cleveland and a graduate of Case Western Unversity came to Simpsonville in 1966 to serve as director of engineering. By 1968 he was plant manager. He and his team, which included motion study engineers, production engineers, and industrial engineers, designed and built automation equipment in house. Unfortunately, recalled one product manager, the earliest generation of engineers did not recognize the importance of training. "They sometimes would wheel equipment out on the floor, say, 'Here it is. This is the way it's supposed to work. Enjoy it,'" and leave it to the people on the floor to figure it out.[30]

KEMET production leadership in 1974 (l to r):
Henry DeMatos (film), Dale Hazen (tantalum),
Harry Holland (group project leader),
Dick Thompson (tantalum chip and micron series),
Sandy Beck (hi-rel), and John Makhijani (ceramic).

continued on page 88

THE QUALITY REVOLUTION

Producing material of consistent quality and being attentive to client needs had long been central to marketing at KEMET. As part of Union Carbide, the company shared its well established approach to building customer relationships and tailoring products for custom applications. But in the 1970s, KEMET embraced a new approach that swept the entire company. The idea seems to have occurred to multiple personnel more or less simultaneously: Erwin Fischler, tantalum project director, and Brian Hawthornthwaite, director of quality, both spoke about encountering the work of W. Edward Deming, who pioneered methods of statistical process control (SPC) as a means of measuring and improving performance, yield, and productivity, and the work of Joseph M. Juran, the consultant who developed managerial protocols that improved industrial efficiency.[31]

The most fundamental insight offered by both Deming and Juran was that waste was reduced and processes improved by focusing on the person rather than the product. KEMET embraced a philosophy of total employee involvement (TEI), emphasizing that all personnel had the ability to identify and solve problems, and make significant contributions to the success of the company. Attention to quality was important not just on the factory floor, but also in packaging, distribution, marketing, billing — every aspect of the company's

Team building exercises at KEMET in the early 1980s fostered a company culture that emphasized the ideals of quality through total employee involvement.

function was open to improvement. Every office in each of KEMET's facilities organized quality circles, devoted to identifying and improving inefficiencies.

The new emphasis paid off handsomely. Instituting statistical controls for process and quality resulted in improved products with extremely low failure rates. For example, by January 1980, KEMET had delivered 6.5 million capacitors to Raytheon for its Hawk Missile program. Statistically, one would expect the defect rate at that level of testing to be 3 percent, but the capacitors KEMET shipped to Raytheon had a defect rate of only 1.2 percent.[32] KEMET's exacting standards have consistently raised the bar for the entire industry. The halls of its facility in Simpsonville are full of trophies and plaques awarded by decades of grateful clients, including Ford, Raytheon, Westinghouse, Honeywell, IBM, and many other leading manufacturers. Ⓚ

A team approach to problem solving at KEMET improved efficiency and built community across the company.

Leading clients have long honored KEMET with vendor awards for the consistent quality of its capacitors.

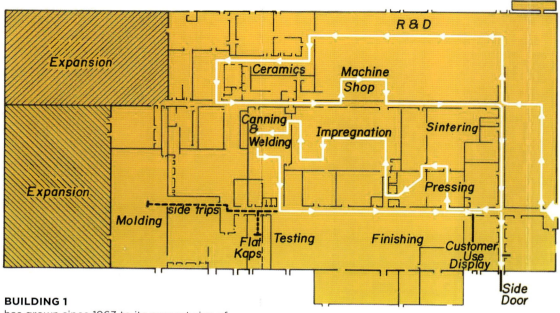

Ten years after establishing a facility in Simpsonville, SC, KEMET expanded its main plant from 40,000 to over 175,000 square feet, and built a second factory.

BUILDING 1
has grown since 1963 to its present size of 177,000 square feet.

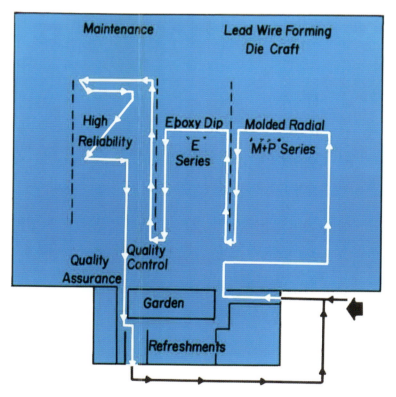

BUILDING 2
was acquired in 1971 when Cleveland facilities were moved to Simpsonville. The plant contains 66,000 square feet of tantalum capacitor production space.

Automating processes not only improved efficiency and production but also allowed KEMET to open plants elsewhere with the assurance that standards of quality would be maintained. In 1968, the company inaugurated its first distant operation, a tantalum capacitor manufacturing plant in Matamoros, Mexico, just over the border from Brownsville, Texas. The move was important not only in terms of expanding operations but also in terms of expanding sales. A number of companies that used KEMET products — notably automotive manufacturers — had established assembly plants in Mexico known locally as maquiladoras. Proximity allowed KEMET to supply some of their key customers at a moment's notice. The company also opened new domestic plants in South Carolina, North Carolina, and Texas. The attention to customer satisfaction and product quality was part of a growing company ethos that made it an eager participant in what is known as "the Quality Revolution."

KEMET was at the top of its game in 1984 when the company was hit by a crisis from an entirely unexpected quarter. A chemical explosion in Bhopal, India killed more than 7,000 people, creating a long lasting environmental disaster. The plant belonged to KEMET's parent company, Union Carbide. Even though KEMET was far removed from the incident and represented a tiny fraction of the massive corporation, company loyalty ran high, and the horror of what happened felt personal. How could Union Carbide have allowed this to happen? Everyone at KEMET was deeply shaken.

As the corporation reeled to contain the disaster overseas, it suffered another hit closer to home. By 1985, Union Carbide was one of the world's largest and most diverse companies, with approximately 700 plants, factories, laboratories, mines, and mills scattered across six continents. Despite this scale, however, its stock was chronically undervalued. Financial analysts frequently remarked that the corporation was too big to be managed properly, and Union Carbide's parts were worth more than the whole.

This was an invitation to corporate raiders, who took advantage of Union Carbide's weakness after Bhopal. The General Aniline & Film (GAF) Corporation launched a bid for a hostile takeover. The stakes were clear: if GAF were to succeed in acquiring Union Carbide, it would strip the corporation's assets bare. "Given that," wrote Union Carbide's CEO in the company newsletter, "your Board of Directors has acted to assure that those Union Carbide businesses to be sold will not be sold hurriedly by people who neither understand nor care about them. We believe it far more desirable to find proper and suitable homes for them so that our employees' and customers' interests are appropriately respected."[33]

There was no getting around it: KEMET would be sold. The only question was: to whom? In order to preserve everything that they had built over the decades, the company needed to find a buyer fast. What Dave Maguire and his team did next surprised everyone, and saved KEMET.

CHAPTER FOUR:
BUILDING A POWERHOUSE

THE DECISION TO ESTABLISH KEMET AS AN INDEPENDENT COMPANY WAS NOT THE first thought. They started by trying to interest other companies in buying the company: "AVX, Sprague, we tried them all," remembers International Sales Manager Don Poinsette. "They all turned us down."[1] The price was too high, and the future too uncertain. So in March 1987, KEMET senior managers, later known as the "Fab Fourteen," organized a leveraged buyout of the company, including the headquarters and plant in Simpsonville, and nine other plants in the United States and Mexico. Under the terms of the sale, Union Carbide would retain 50 percent interest in the company, the management would own 15 percent, and GE would own 35 percent. Dave Maguire was appointed as the first CEO, and Charles "Chuck" Volpe as executive vice president. KEMET's long relationship with Union Carbide allowed the new company to make as smooth a transition as possible.

Managers at KEMET, including Bob Taylor, Chuck Volpe, Dan Manley, and Dave Maguire, look on as a client representative signs a contract.

The first steps after independence were to establish crucial infrastructure. Like other subsidiaries, KEMET had depended on the parent corporation for certain essential functions, including managing taxes and other financial matters, organizing employee benefits, and providing office space necessary for roles, such as sales. Jim Jerozal came to KEMET directly from Union Carbide at the time of the buyout to serve as chief financial officer, bringing a wealth of experience that would help structure the company's financial independence. Although KEMET had its own sales team — necessary given the highly technical nature of the electronics field — they had always been able to rely upon Union Carbide's ample facilities. Between 1987 and 1989, KEMET established six regional sales offices and 19 district offices across the continental United States and Puerto Rico. At the same time, the company opened new international sales offices in Switzerland, England, Germany, France, Hong Kong, Singapore, and China, and renegotiated contracts for sales representatives in nine other countries. KEMET's products were shipped overseas from its major distribution facility in Atlanta, Georgia, while Amsterdam served as the major hub for international distribution to both Europe and Asia, with smaller distribution facilities located in England, France, Italy, Switzerland, Germany, Norway, Sweden, Hong Kong, and Singapore.

1987
KEMET's senior managers organize a leveraged buyout from Union Carbide, establishing KEMET as an independent company.

1992
KEMET becomes a publicly traded company.

2000
KEMET's sales exceed $1 billion for the first time.

2003
KEMET opens its first Asian plant, in Suzhou, China. Others will follow in Japan, Vietnam, and Thailand.

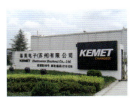

2005
Per-Olof Loof joins KEMET as the new CEO.

2006
KEMET acquires EPCOS Tantalum.

2007
KEMET acquires Evox Rifa.

2007
KEMET acquires Arcotronics.

2012
KEMET acquires Niotan Incorporated, renaming it KEMET Blue Powder.

2012
KEMET launches partnership to produce conflict-free tantalum in the Democratic Republic of Congo.

2017
KEMET acquires NEC TOKIN and renames it TOKIN.

THE FAB F

KEMET'S TOP MANAGERS SAVED THE COMPANY WITH A LEVERAGED BUYOUT FROM UNION CARBIDE IN APRIL 1987

DAVID E. MAGUIRE

President and CEO, received a degree in mathematics and industrial engineering from the University of Michigan and would spend virtually his entire career at KEMET, rising from project engineer to vice president of the company under Union Carbide.

CHARLES E. VOLPE

Executive vice president, received a degree in mechanical engineering from Rochester Institute of Technology. After a stint at Honeywell, he joined KEMET as a sales engineer in 1966. In 1995 he would succeed Maguire as president and chief operating officer. After retirement, he devoted himself to philanthropy in the arts and medicine.

JAMES JEROZAL

Chief financial officer, joined Union Carbide as an administrator manager shortly after he received a degree in accounting from DePaul University in 1968. He joined KEMET at the time of the sale from Union Carbide, where he had served 12 years as controller of the electronics division.

BRIAN G. HAWTHORNTHWAITE

Vice president of quality, received a degree in electrical engineering from Clemson University in 1963. After a brief stint at DuPont, he joined KEMET to design equipment to automate key processes. After serving for 10 years as a quality manager, he was lured to the Juran Institute in 1986 to serve as a vice president. At Maguire's request, Hawthornthwaite returned in 1987 to help with the buyout.

BERND K. SCHEUMANN

Domestic manufacturing manager, received his training in mechanical engineering at the University of Frankfurt. After 14 years with ITT in Nuremberg, Germany, he came to work at KEMET in 1981 to lead the tantalum group. By 1986, he was operations manager for tantalum and ceramics.

DONALD A. ADAMS

Mexico manufacturing manager, received a degree in chemistry and mathematics from Franklin College of Indiana in 1967. He went to work for P. R. Mallory, an electrolytic capacitor manufacturer, and Duracell batteries, helping to establish their operations in Mexico. When Mallory was sold in 1977, Adams joined KEMET, serving in increasingly senior managerial roles in the company's plant in Matamoros.

GLENN H. SPEARS

Vice president of human resources, graduated from Auburn University in 1961 with a degree in mechanical engineering.  After 13 years at DuPont and two years as an independent consultant, he joined KEMET in 1977 as a process engineer in the tantalum division. Two years later he was plant manager, and soon after that director of human relations. In 1999, he would be promoted to executive vice president and secretary.

DR. JOHN PIPER

Vice president of technology, was born in London and came to the United States as a teenager to study chemistry at Trinity College, Connecticut and MIT, where he earned a Ph.D. in 1960. 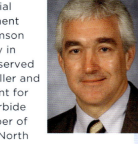 He started as a research chemist in Union Carbide's labs in Tarrytown, NY. In 1967, he moved to South Carolina to lead KEMET's program in ceramics, but soon expanded his duties to manage the company's scientific research.

D. RAY CASH

Vice president of administration, earned a degree in industrial management from Clemson University in 1970. He served as controller and accountant for Union Carbide in a number of states — North Carolina, Arkansas, Illinois, Connecticut, and New Jersey — before coming home to South Carolina, and KEMET, in 1985. In 2000, he would succeed Jerozal as chief financial officer.

KENNETH L. MARTIN

Vice president of engineering, received his degree in chemical engineering from Kansas State University in 1964. Before joining KEMET in 1986 as director of engineering, he spent the bulk of his career as an operations manager at Texas Instruments, with earlier stints at Westinghouse and Mobil.

ROBERT A. TAYLOR

National sales manager, served in the Army Reserve while obtaining an associate degree at Presbyterian Junior College in 1961. He spent five years at KEMET in various roles — 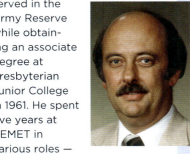 inspection supervisor, shipping supervisor, quality assurance manager — before discovering a talent for sales. By 1973 he was regional sales manager for the Southeast, and by 1983, he was in charge of KEMET's sales nationwide.

ED BOST

Product marketing manager, served in the Navy before attending Clemson University, where he obtained a master's degree in ceramic engineering in 1963. After  several years of research at the Atomic Energy Commission and elsewhere, he worked as an engineer in tantalum, a superintendent in ceramic chip manufacturing, and a plant manager at KEMET's facility in Columbus, GA, before becoming marketing manager.

HARRIS L. CROWLEY

Product marketing manager, served in Vietnam before securing a degree in ceramic engineering from Clemson University in 1975. He joined Union Carbide immediately  after his discharge from school, working first as a production engineer for the Linde division in Mobile, AL. In 1978, he came to KEMET to work in production first in tantalum, then in ceramic products. In 1999 he was named a senior vice president for technology and engineering.

DONALD J. POINSETTE

International sales manager, joined Union Carbide soon after he received his degree in industrial economics from Purdue University in 1963. He served the corporation in a number of posts across several divisions, ranging from New York to Chicago to Buenos Aires. In 1980, he moved to South Carolina to lead KEMET's international sales team.

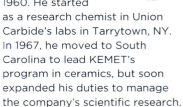

The new KEMET, built by the Fab Fourteen and over 6,000 worldwide employees was off to a strong start and getting stronger. In 1977, KEMET's sales accounted for 35 percent of the market for tantalum capacitors, and 11 percent of the market for ceramics. By 1988, KEMET had 44 percent of the tantalum market and 21 percent of the ceramic market, and by 1989 the company was outperforming its major competitors, AVX and Sprague Electric, which had higher volumes of sales but much narrower profit margins.

There were three main factors that led to KEMET's early success. First was its focus on the high reliability (hi-rel) market. Although the company continued to produce ample materials for commercial off-the-shelf sales by nationwide distributors, customized products for special applications by original equipment manufacturers (OEMs) made up a substantial proportion of KEMET's sales. In 1989, the top 50 customers accounted for 72 percent ($188.7 million) of the company's total sales of $261.7 million (about $530 million in 2019 dollars). Distributors such as TTI, Hamilton/Avnet, and Schweber were at the top, with $53.4 million in combined annual sales. Next came computer manufacturers such as IBM, Hewlett-Packard, and Western Digital ($43.7 million combined annual sales), communications companies such as AT&T and Motorola ($37 million), automotive companies such as General Motors (GM) and Ford ($26.4 million), defense contractors such as Honeywell and Raytheon ($21.6 million), and companies specializing in industrial applications such as Rockwell and Xerox ($6.7 million).[2]

Examples of customized applications from these early years of KEMET's independence are numerous. When IBM wanted a capacitor that could not be inserted incorrectly (which can cause catastrophic failure), KEMET designed a prototype three-lead capacitor in two weeks, and was in full production in three weeks. GM experienced dramatic

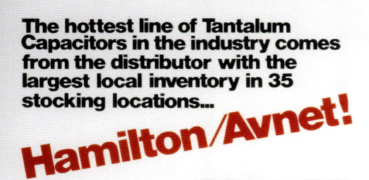

Founded in 1921, the electronics distributor Avnet has been one of KEMET's most important clients since the late 1950s. This ad dates from the early 1980s, when the company — then called Hamilton/Avnet — teamed up with KEMET to power the PC revolution.

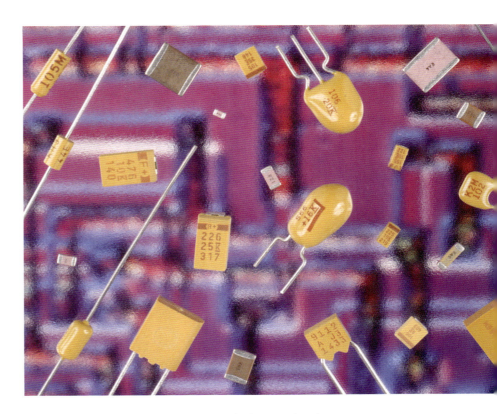

KEMET capacitors powered personal computer and peripherals produced by IBM, Hewlett-Packard, Western Digital, and other leading manufacturers.

disasters with several vehicles when electronic components placed too close to the engine block caught fire. In response, KEMET designed surface-mount capacitors that could withstand the high temperatures GM's cars generated. KEMET's long term agreement with Hewlett-Packard led it to supply all of the tantalum chips used in Palm Pilots, the first handheld computing device.

KEMET's devotion to customer satisfaction was amply repaid. The company regularly received annual customer quality awards from AT&T, Compaq, Data General, GE, GM, Hughes Aircraft, Honeywell, IBM, ITT, Motorola, Raytheon, Teledyne, and many other manufacturers who depended on KEMET's products. In 1994, Ford purchased parts from 5,500 external suppliers; of these only 27 were awarded the automaker's prestigious Total Quality Excellence Award. KEMET was one of them.[3] Loyalty from companies such as these helped KEMET to weather the economic storms that were to come in the 1990s and early 2000s.

VP of Quality Brian Hawthornthwaite (left) and Ford KKAT Leader Johnny Boan (right) complete the first step towards winning the 1994 Ford Total Quality Excellence Award.

SURFACE-MOUNT TANTALUM CAPACITORS

Developed after the leaded tantalum capacitor and the multilayer ceramic capacitor (see page 69), the surface-mount tantalum capacitor operates on similar principles. The major variance here is that the anode and cathode terminals are in the form of surfaces that might be mounted directly to a circuit board. Whereas tantalum capacitors traditionally had relied on manganese dioxide (MnO_2) to serve as the electrodes, KEMET's products now typically use a conductive polymer developed in the 1980s and 1990s by the NEC Corporation. The polymer offers lower resistance and operates at a lower voltage than MnO_2 and is optimal for use in digital circuits.[4]

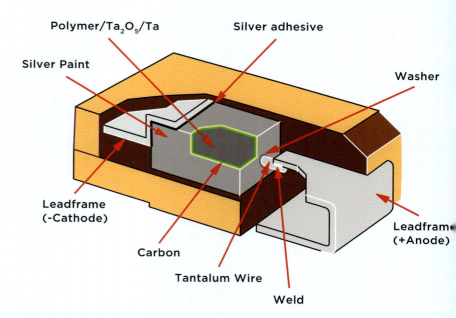

In 1998, KEMET entered into a licensing agreement with NEC for the joint development of high performance, conductive, polymer tantalum capacitors marketed under the name KO-CAP®. The agreement was the brainchild of Charles M. Culbertson II, who led the tantalum product line and would later become KEMET's chief operating officer. The company's new T510 series also introduced a market innovation: a product with multiple capacitor elements positioned in parallel that could offer the lowest electrical resistance in the industry.[5] **K**

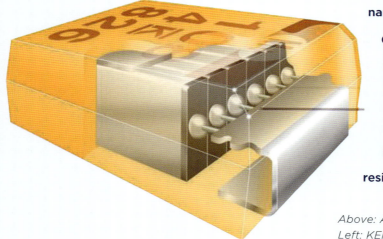

Above: Anatomy of a prototypical, surface-mount tantalum capacitor. Left: KEMET's groundbreaking T510 series, introduced in 1998, set a new standard for tantalum capacitors.

The second ingredient for KEMET's growth was increasing its investment in surface-mount technology, essential as consumer electronics continued to get smaller and more powerful. Today, surface-mounted devices (SMDs) are ubiquitous. They are more compact than leaded devices, fitting on both sides of a circuit board, and thus offer the "real estate advantage" critical for miniaturization. Since they are soldered directly onto the circuit board rather than threaded through holes, SMDs also lend themselves more easily to automated applications, reducing assembly time and cost. But the electronics industry was very skeptical at first. For one thing, at the beginning there were no uniform standards for SMDs with regard to either capacitance or size. Furthermore, SMDs required entirely new industrial processes and equipment to manufacture. Deploying them required the original equipment manufacturers (OEMs) who used capacitors to retool their operations as well. But no one in the electronics industry was confident that OEMs would make use of the new technology. As late as the early 1990s, industry analysts thought it unlikely that companies would invest the millions of dollars required to convert their leaded applications to SMDs.

But KEMET recognized the promise of tantalum SMDs as early as the 1970s. In 1971, the company's chief scientist John Piper lamented that "tantalum chips would be preferable" to leaded components, "but have not been practicable" due to certain complications that had not yet been worked out.[6] Between 1981 and 1991, the company invested $50 million in machinery and equipment to produce surface-mounted chips. KEMET's surface-mounted products fed the computer boom of the 1980s. Over the next decade KEMET would triple its investment, quickly establishing itself as the world's leading supplier of tantalum SMDs. Never satisfied to rest on its laurels, the company developed a new high stress application test in 1987 to improve the performance of hybrid ceramic chips. Rigorous application and experimentation allowed KEMET to bring the failure rate down from 50,000 parts per million (PPM) in 1987 to 500 PPM by the end of 1989.

The third ingredient for KEMET's success was what every employee at the time would identify as the most important: a company-wide embrace of five core values that applied to everyone from the mail room to the board room. The ethos of total employee involvement that was at the core of the quality revolution permeated every corner of the company, thanks in large part to the vision of Brian Hawthornthwaite. "When Rockwell officials came to KEMET recently to discuss the implementation of a ship-to-stock program," wrote one manager in 1989, "production workers were brought in off the manufacturing floor to share their thoughts on improving quality levels to eliminate the need for incoming inspection."[7] The company-wide devotion to quality, technology, and savings was matched only by its commitment to customer service. "Their customer obsession is unique," enthused a financial analyst at Merrill Lynch. "There's nobody else like KEMET."[8]

One of KEMET's techniques for maintaining high standards of efficiency and quality and controlling costs was through focusing its plants on specific products. By 1989, the company had factories in six cities. In Simpsonville, SC, the company had two facilities for tantalum capacitors, and another for high reliability ceramic capacitors. In Mauldin, SC, KEMET manufactured surface-mount tantalum chips; in Columbus, GA, axial molded tantalum; in Greenwood, SC, radial dipped tantalum. There were ceramic plants in Shelby, NC, and Fountain Inn, SC. Among the most important of KEMET's factories was the one in Matamoros, Mexico, just over the border from Brownsville, TX. Founded in 1967 — only four years after the move to Greenville, SC, — and in operation since 1969, KEMET de México would expand to include plants in Monterrey and Ciudad Victoria, and serve as one of the major hubs for the company's assembly and manufacturing operations.

KEMET's strong growth made its managers confident when Union Carbide announced its decision in 1990 to divest itself of its 50 percent ownership stake in the company. The corporation was still reeling from the fallout of the Bhopal disaster, facing extraordinary fines and calls for criminal prosecution — the government of India had issued an arrest warrant for Union Carbide's CEO Warren Anderson, who was formally declared a fugitive from justice. The company needed to raise capital. (By 1999 Union Carbide would collapse completely, selling its remaining core assets to Dow.) Forming a partnership with Citicorp Venture Capital, Heller Financial, and the Westinghouse Credit Corporation, KEMET's managers bought the remainder of Union Carbide's stake for $235 million (over $450 million in 2019 dollars).[9] KEMET's ability to operate successfully despite its heavily leveraged status (it had taken on significant debt to finance the initial buyout) had attracted these new backers, who saw its size, reputation, and steadily widening margins as indicative of a promising future as a publicly traded company.

continued on page 102

KEMET'S FIVE CORE VALUES

**AS A NEW COMPANY, KEMET INTRODUCED FIVE CORE VALUES
THAT SERVED AS GUIDELINES FOR EXCELLENCE**

1 **BEST TRAINED AND MOTIVATED PEOPLE**
*Commitment to employee growth and satisfaction,
environmental stewardship, and corporate citizenship*

2 **COMPANY-WIDE QUALITY CONCEPT**
*A management process aimed at establishing
a distinctive competence that differentiates
KEMET as the unquestioned best-in-class supplier*

3 **EASY TO BUY FROM**
*Commitment to total customer satisfaction,
with systems in place to facilitate ordering
and distribution*

4 **LOWEST COST PRODUCER**
*Continuous quest to develop cost-efficient
manufacturing equipment and processes*

5 **LEADING EDGE OF TECHNOLOGY**
*A permanent investment in research and
development*

KEMET DE MÉXICO

KEMET was among the first wave of companies to establish maquiladoras (processing plants) in Matamoros, Mexico, between 1966 and 1970. The move was made possible by the Border Industrialization Program (BIP) instituted by the government of Mexico in 1965 as a means of combating widespread unemployment. The BIP allowed for the unrestricted entry of foreign capital into the region, and afforded duty and tax preferences

to companies that operated there. The result was a boom in the local economy, with dozens of American automotive and electronics companies setting up factories that would employ thousands.

Opening a plant in Mexico afforded the company some obvious advantages. The country had an abundant and well organized labor force — most KEMET employees in Mexico are proud members of the Confederación de Trabajadores de Mexico. Wage differentials between the United States and Mexico also allowed the company to keep costs down. Equally important was the fact that other companies took advantage of the BIP. KEMET found itself at the center of a growing regional hub of manufacturing companies that relied on capacitors: other pioneers in the region included GE, Zenith Electronics, and Delphi Delco, which specialized in automotive electronics. This proximity to some of KEMET's most important customers allowed them to fulfill rush orders quickly and facilitated collaboration on innovative products. Matamoros, the location of KEMET's first plant in Mexico, is located just over the border from Brownsville, TX.

KEMET's first factory in Matamoros introduced the world to the company's first line of ceramic products.

KEMET's new factories in Ciudad Victoria (top) and Monterrey (middle) house state-of-the-art facilities within a structures that pay homage to local architectural traditions.

Bottom: KEMET's personnel in Mexico work with ground-breaking equipment to produce capacitors used worldwide.

Brownsville itself became a vital distribution hub for the company, supplying Southwestern Bell as well as the high tech industries that were growing quickly in Texas and California.

In 1969, KEMET de México focused on assembling the company's brand new line of multilayer ceramic capacitors, introducing the world to what would long serve one of the company's most important products. Over time KEMET's operations in Matamoros would grow to four plants totaling 234,000 square feet. In 1989, the company began construction on a plant in Monterrey, Mexico, which commenced operations in 1991. In 1997, KEMET started a second plant in Monterrey. In 1998, KEMET initiated a tantalum manufacturing plant in Ciudad Victoria that was in operation by September 1999.

Today, the company has almost 6,000 employees in Mexico, with stellar safety records and high rates of job satisfaction, exemplified by a much lower-than-average rate of employee turnover for the region. Like their United States operations, KEMET's Mexico operations have won numerous quality awards from their customers. The company would not be what it is today without KEMET de México. **K**

KEMET's first Board of Directors as a publicly traded company (left to right): E. Erwin Maddrey II, Charles E. Volpe, David E. Maguire, Steven L. Gerard, Stewart A. Kohl.

On October 21, 1992, KEMET went public, joining the Nasdaq Exchange at $10 a share.[10] The board of directors included CEO Dave Maguire and COO Chuck Volpe. Joining them were three collaborators who brought considerable experience and expertise: E. Erwin Maddrey II, CEO of Delta Woodside Industries, a textile company with deep roots in South Carolina; Steven L. Gerard, CEO of Triangle Wire & Cable, a leading supplier to the electronics industry; and Stewart A. Kohl, vice president at Citicorp who had convinced the bank to invest in KEMET. Gerard cycled off the board after only a few years, while Kohl, later the co-CEO of Riverside, a private equity company, would serve on the board until 2005. Maddrey was in it for the long haul, seeing the company through several cycles of boom and bust. By the end of KEMET's first fiscal year as an independent company, they could report sales of nearly $350 million (around $626 million in 2019 dollars) — a record high representing an increase of 18 percent from its final year as a private company. Record sales figures became a recurring pattern in the years that followed: $385 million in 1994, $473 million in 1995, and $634 million in 1996. In four years the company's earnings had increasec fivefold.[11]

IMPROVING CONDITIONS

Born in San Luis Potosi, Mexico, in 1944, Maria Guadalupe Torres was raised by a single mother who worked as a maid. Torres followed her mother into domestic service. In her early twenties, she found her first industrial job, at a pottery factory just over the border from where she was living in Brownsville, TX. In 1969, she took a position at the new KEMET plant in Matamoros where she earned the nickname "Lupita Epoxy," in honor of her work preparing adhesives. American companies had only recently started opening operations in Mexico. Although standards to ensure the safety of English-speaking employees were in place, more accessible health measures had not been adapted. Notably, at one stage of production, capacitors are washed in methylene chloride, a solvent widely used in industrial processes that must be handled with extreme caution. Warning labels were all in English, and unintelligible to workers who spoke only Spanish. In 1981, Torres led a campaign to improve safety conditions at KEMET, and succeeded in instituting practices that benefitted all of her coworkers — including health and safety training programs in Spanish. In 1987, she left the company to work for the Comité Fronterizo de Obreras, (Borderlands Women Workers Committee), where she would help women at other maquiladoras accomplish what she had done for her coworkers at KEMET. In 2001 Torres was honored by the Texas Civil Rights Project.[12] **K**

After working to improve conditions at KEMET's plant in Matamoros, Maria Guadalupe Torres went on to organize workers at other maquiladoras.

KEMET's financial strength grew from its strong infrastructure, with a well organized production network. A dedicated marketing team worked to develop long term partnerships with a number of important clients, including distributors that served to help KEMET products reach the general market. Among these partnerships, the most important over the years has been with TTI, Inc., an electronic components distributor headquartered in Fort Worth, TX. Founded by Paul Andrews as Tex-Tronics in 1971, TTI now has 100 locations throughout North America, Europe, Asia, and Israel. The two companies matured together, sharing not only a common focus but also a common ethos in their commitment to customer fulfillment and total quality management. It is a mark of the depth of their mutual appreciation that TTI has graced KEMET with its Supplier Excellence Awards every year since the distributor inaugurated the program in 1995.

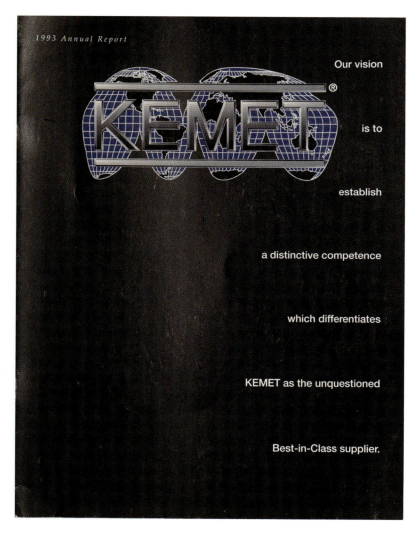

KEMET's first annual report, covering fiscal year 1992.

An exploding market for consumer electronics was the primary driver of KEMET's rapid growth. The microprocessor revolution that had produced the first personal computers in the late 1970s had matured into a burgeoning ecosystem of products powered by microchips, including portable phones and a host of peripheral devices — keyboards, mice, monitors, modems, scanners, disc drives, printers, and the like. Continued growth in automotive electronics also raised demand for KEMET's products. For example, when GM first introduced airbags in the early 1970s, they were counted as a luxury item included only in government fleet vehicles. In the late 1980s, Chrysler made driver-side airbags standard in its cars. In the 1990s, airbag use became widespread. KEMET's products were there at every stage of the airbag's development.

The company had long made specialty medical products for Medtronics and other manufacturers of pacemakers and defibrillators — the reliability of capacitors in these settings was literally a matter of life and death.

KEMET's contributions to the expanding high tech dimensions of daily life were paralleled by special assignments for extraordinary projects. Since its first venture beyond the stratosphere with Telstar in 1962, the company had regularly produced high reliability capacitors for NASA projects, including the Gemini and Apollo missions to the moon, the Viking mission to Mars, the Hubble Space Telescope, the Pathfinder probe, and the Sojourner rover. In 1997, KEMET was tapped to supply capacitors to repair the Russian space station Mir, which was damaged after a collision with an unmanned module. They chose the T110 series, which has a statistically infinite lifespan and can withstand temperatures below -150°C. "KEMET's capacitors provide the electronic reliability necessary for the success of important projects like this," the company's president noted with pride.[13] Later KEMET would supply components for the International Space Station, launched in 1998.

With business booming and KEMET growing steadily, Dave Maguire relinquished the presidency in October 1995 to Chuck Volpe, who had risen from sales engineer to chief operating officer over the course of three decades with the company. Maguire retained his position as CEO and chairman of the board. Health concerns led Volpe to retire in March 1996. He was replaced by Terry R. Weaver, who had joined the company the previous year to serve as vice president of sales and marketing. Weaver would not last long, however, and resigned in November 1997. Maguire returned to assume the presidency, a move that hardly surprised business analysts. Maguire was a "wee bit of a one-man show to a degree," observed John Patrick, a consultant with Herzog Heine Geduld in New York.[14]

Although KEMET had built a very strong business — the company was manufacturing, testing, and selling over 65 million capacitors a day — a rotating executive suite led other corporations to sense an opportunity.[15] In June 1996, just a few months into Weaver's tenure as president,

continued on page 110

THE MICROPROCESSOR REVOLUTION

KEMET worked closely with equipment manufacturers to develop miniature components for the first generation of mobile phones and other handheld devices that defined a new era in electronics.

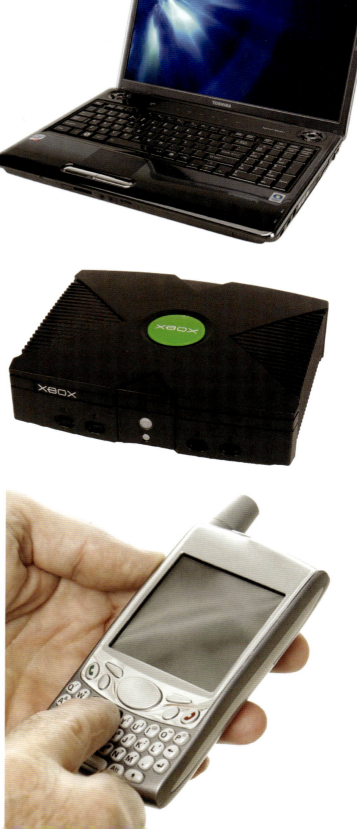

KEMET capacitors power mobile phones, handheld and gaming devices, and other products of the microprocessor revolution.

AUTOMOTIVE SAFETY

Long a key supplier to the industry, KEMET has designed components for airbag systems, power trains, and other crucial automotive electronics. Today, KEMET is helping to develop sensors, charging pads, and other materials to power a new generation of electric and hybrid vehicles.

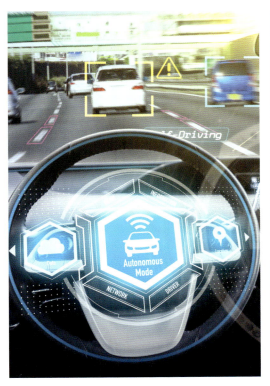

KEMET is a longstanding, trusted supplier of components for the automotive industry.

MEDICAL

In the old days, KEMET developed getters for use in X-ray tubes. Today, the company's products serve as key components in a wide range of medical devices, from pacemakers to magnetic resonance imaging scanners, where reliability and accuracy is essential.

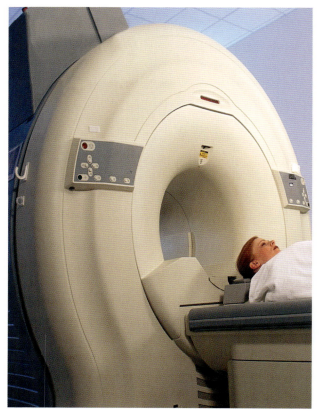

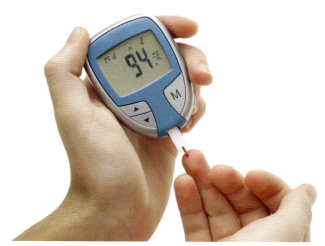

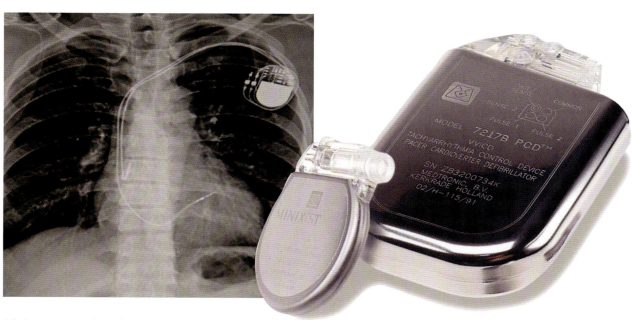

Miniature capacitors by KEMET ensure the efficient operation of pacemakers and other life saving medical devices.

AEROSPACE

KEMET products have been key components of critical space missions since 1962. Designed to last forever, KEMET capacitors power satellites, space telescopes, space stations, and missions to the moon, Mars, and beyond. Airplanes have relied on KEMET components for radar and other electronic systems since the 1940s.

KEMET has produced high reliabilty capacitors for many defense and aerospace projects, including the International Space Station.

Vishay Intertechnology made a serious and much publicized bid to purchase KEMET (for nearly one billion dollars). Four years earlier, Vishay had purchased the tantalum capacitor operations of Sprague Electric, KEMET's longtime competitor. Acquiring KEMET would have allowed the company to control almost half of the global market in capacitors. It was an attractive offer, but KEMET declined the offer quickly. "KEMET is not interested in engaging in discussions," said Glenn Spears, senior vice president and secretary of the board.[16] Vishay continued to pursue the deal, announcing its offer — $22 a share, or about $850 million in total — and urging stockholders to lobby management to sell. "Maybe they will change their mind, maybe something else will happen," said Vishay's CEO. But KEMET held firm, its resolve demonstrating to investors and market watchers that its managers were supremely confident in the company's future.[17]

The game of musical chairs at the top of KEMET's corporate structure came at a time when the market was on the brink of a seismic shift. The electronics industry is notoriously volatile — technological breakthroughs continuously change the nature of the field, rendering popular products and established companies obsolete overnight. Companies that supply basic components such as KEMET are relatively well positioned to take advantage of the opportunities offered by innovation, but they take a hit when their customers experience a decline in demand. Such downturns in the broader electronics market in 1985 and 1989 compelled KEMET to lay off workers. In 1992 KEMET closed its plant in Georgia that specialized in leaded tantalum capacitors that the company's surface-mount products were rendering obsolete.

The other major risk factor involves inventory. While component manufacturers may be tempted to ramp up production during boom times, they must be careful not to overproduce. Similarly, original equipment manufacturers (OEMs) who purchase components must be careful not to overbuy on the basis of estimated demand for their products. As one market report noted in 1990, "Over the past 30 years, excessive inventory buildups have been the bane of the industry."[18] A notorious example in the capacitor industry occurred between 1968 and 1970 when Japanese firms flooded the market with aluminum electrolytic capacitors sold at cost or below. Although KEMET was not affected that time, many of its competitors suffered and initiated an anti-dumping suit with the Tariff Commission. Over the following years, KEMET was repeatedly compelled to lay off and rehire workers in keeping with these economic cycles. In the fiscal year ending in March 1997, KEMET would experience another "correction cycle" where inventory buildup would result in a 13 percent drop in sales. Things would get worse.

Electronic News

VOL. 42 • NO. 2124　　　　　　　　　　　　　　MONDAY JULY 8, 1996 • TWO DOLLARS

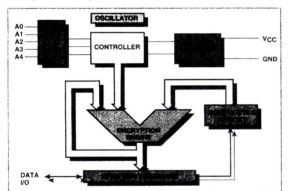

Based on Nanoteq's Keeloq hopping-code technology, the XL107 SureLok from Exel Microelectronics generates random algorithms for a virtually unbreakable security system. The 8-pin chip is designed to be embedded in keys, smart cards, battery packs and computer add-in cards. Currently in volume production, the XL107 is priced starting at $0.94 each in 1,000-unit quantities. See story, page 70.

DEC To Disappoint In 4Q; PC Business, Europe Cited

BY ELAINE CHEN

MAYNARD, MASS.—Despite growing success for the Alpha microprocessor, Digital Equipment continues to struggle, disclosing lower than expected 4Q results and major job cuts only one day after launching an ambitious Alpha roadmap. Digital also announced the resignation of Enrico Pesatori, VP and GM of the Computer Systems division.

Continued losses in the PC business, along with a weak European market, were cited as leading factors in Digital's woes. "We have disappointed ourselves in the last two quarters," said Digital CEO Robert Palmer. "Where we are today is not where we intended to be."

Analysts agree that retrenchment continues to be necessary, with costs at Digital still too high despite years of cutbacks. While analysts continue to find hope in its Windows NT

CONTINUED ON PAGE 86

KEMET's rejection of a strong takeover bid signaled confidence to investors.

In Bid For New Markets
Rockwell To Buy Brooktree

BY ANDREW MACLELLAN

SEAL BEACH, CALIF.—Rockwell International moved to acquire San Diego-based Brooktree Corp. in a $275 million stock transaction, a deal which observers believe could help Rockwell solidify its digital and mixed-signal communications product line and expand its presence in the multimedia arena.

Pending government and shareholder approval, Brooktree, which had FY95 sales of $138 million, will become a wholly-owned subsidiary of Rockwell and will operate as a division of Rockwell Semiconductor Systems.

Dataquest senior analyst Dave Ford called the bid a strategic one which will help Rockwell re-tool its image as a provider of fax/modem and wireless communications components to reflect the market's larger potential.

> ### ANALOG DEVICES BUYS MOSAIC MICROSYSTEMS
> ### SEE PAGE 4

"The bottom line is it's a complementary thing that really moves Rockwell along in its efforts to enter the realm of personal communications," said Mr. Ford. "Brooktree brings two things, digital communications, and, of course, a graphics capability. And that's really a completely new capability Rockwell acquires here."

Under the agreement, Brooktree's 575 employees will be retained. Operations in San Diego, Colorado and Texas will remain open and could be expanded. Brooktree's sales efforts in Asia and Europe and a product test facility in Singapore also will continue largely unaffected, although the companies' sales forces face future consolidation.

"From a management standpoint, we will merge into one cohesive entity, but the determination as to where our resources are to be deployed has yet to be made," said Brooktree president/CEO James A. Bixby, who reported that the company's shareholders have so far reacted favorably to the acquisition plan. On

CONTINUED ON PAGE 92

KEMET TO VISHAY: NO WAY

BY BERNARD LEVINE

GREENVILLE, S.C.—Capacitor maker Kemet Electronics spurned Vishay Intertechnology's take-over initiative (EN, July 1), telling its suitor early last week it was "not interested in engaging in discussions." Kemet's board also implemented poison pill provisions that would make any hostile Vishay tender offer for Kemet difficult.

Vishay had not responded by the start of the long holiday weekend, with its chairman, Felix Zandman, apparently still weighing whether to proceed on an unfriendly basis or throw in the towel. Dr. Zandman had earlier proposed "friendly discussions regarding a merger of the two companies" in a letter to Kemet chairman David Maguire. Neither Dr. Zandman nor Mr. Maguire has returned phone calls seeking comment since the take-over saga between the passive component powerhouses began.

Other Vishay officials have also been unavailable, but Glenn Spears, Kemet senior VP and secretary of the board, was reached on Wednesday. "At this time, the statement we released on Monday sums up our position

CONTINUED ON PAGE 90

The devaluation of the Thai baht in July 1997 launched a series of financial aftershocks across Asia that had worldwide repercussions. Speculative bubbles popped in Indonesia, Philippines, Malaysia and South Korea; Japan, whose banks had been struggling, slid into its worst recession in 50 years. The effects of the Asian Financial Crisis were felt in many sectors; KEMET and electronic manufacturers saw their exports to Asia drastically reduced. At the same time, the recent phasing out of protective tariffs encouraged Asian manufacturers to bring their inventory to the US market, resulting in an excess of products made especially cheap thanks to exporters' currency devaluations relative to the US dollar. To make matters worse, the price of palladium, a rare metal essential to the production of ceramic capacitors, tripled to a 20-year high of $1,090 per troy ounce.[19] Worldwide sales of surface-mount tantalum and ceramic capacitors, which accounted for over 80 percent of KEMET's business, plummeted. Net earnings dropped from $49 million in fiscal year 1998 to just $6 million in fiscal 1999. Facing disaster, company managers made tough but necessary decisions, laying off workers, closing plants, and moving key operations to the new facility in Ciudad Victoria, Mexico. KEMET personnel would later recall these times as "the Dark Years," but everyone understood that these measures were what was required to survive.

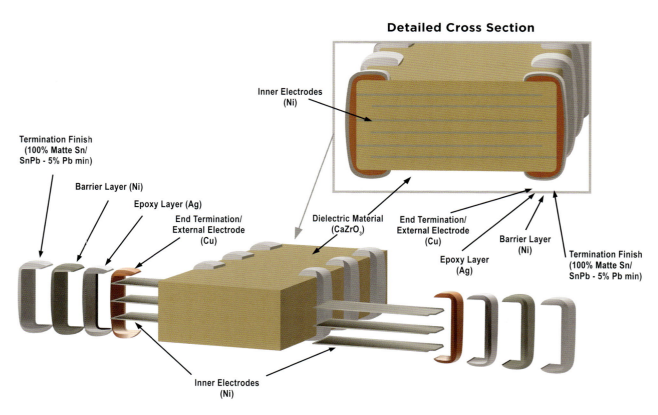

Necessity during the Asian financial crisis drove KEMET to invent a more efficient and cheaper ceramic capacitor.

It is to KEMET's credit that what was one of the most trying times in its history was also one of its most innovative. Company engineers knew that the broader economic crisis would not slow the pace of advancements in computing, the engine of KEMET's business. The processing power of integrated circuits continued to double about every 18 months. Even while struggling to stay afloat, KEMET never ceased looking towards the future. In response to skyrocketing palladium prices, ceramic engineers developed the Base Metal Electrode (BME), one that replaced this expensive material with nickel, with no reduction in capacitance or quality. Reaching across the international divide, KEMET forged a deal with a Japanese competitor, the NEC Corporation, for the joint development of polymer tantalum capacitors which KEMET marketed under the name KO-CAP®. They would become one of the company's signature products in the decades to come.

Skittish investors heaved a collective sigh of relief when Charles M. Culbertson II was promoted to the presidency in June 1999. A graduate of Clemson University, Culbertson joined KEMET in 1980, and had recently served as manager of the company's Maudlin plant and as senior vice president and general manager of KEMET's tantalum business unit. It was he who had brokered the deal with NEC. Even though Maguire continued as CEO, it was

Charles Culbertson brokered the cooperative arrangement with NEC Corporation that lead to the development of KO-CAPs®.

widely expected that Culbertson's promotion established a clear line of succession. "Culbertson has run both sides of the business and knows it as well as anybody," observed an analyst with J. P. Morgan. "[His promotion] answers a question the investment community has had. Not a burning one, but one that always comes up when you talk about KEMET."[20]

Culbertson's appointment coincided with a rush of financial speculation centered on the Internet that would later be termed the "dot-com bubble." Overnight it appeared that the company's fortunes had changed. KEMET's stock, which had been listed on the Nasdaq since October 1992, moved to the New York Stock Exchange (NYSE) in December 1999, significantly raising its profile with investors worldwide. In January 2000, the company completed a public offering of 5.8 million shares of common stock at $46 per share. In the fiscal year ending in March 2000, KEMET posted records sales of $822 million (about $1.2 billion in 2019 dollars), up 45 percent over 1999. On December 11, 2000, annual earnings exceeded $1 billion (almost $1.5 billion in 2019 dollars) for the first time in the company's history. At their annual meeting, the company's shareholders greeted Maguire with a standing ovation.

But it was not to last. The dot-com bubble had been fueled by what Federal Reserve chairman Alan Greenspan called "irrational exuberance," and on March 11, 2001 it finally burst. Electronics manufacturers and telecom companies, which had been racing ahead of their expectations, suddenly found themselves unable to live up to their promises. Throughout most of fiscal 2002, overstocked telecom buyers reduced their orders by nearly half. KEMET's net sales plummeted from $1.4 billion (almost $2 billion in 2019 dollars) in FY 2001 to $509 million in FY 2002; net earnings for the first time in the company's history were in the negatives: a $27.3 million loss. "In my forty-three years at KEMET, spanning eleven industry cycles," David Maguire wrote to shareholders that year, "I have never experienced a correction of this magnitude and rapidity."[21] Once again, the company was forced to reduce its workforce, but this time the measure was truly devastating. From June 2000 to March 2002, the employee base was reduced from 16,000 to 6,900. On January 23, 2002, Culbertson stepped down as president. Despite everything, the company maintained the same, standards of quality as ever. In January 2002, Northrup Grumman awarded KEMET its highest award for suppliers.

KEMET's managers framed the weekly financial statement marking the company's first billion.

Dr. Jeffrey Graves had left GE in 2001 to join KEMET as vice president of technology. In October 2002, he rose to fill Culbertson's place as president and chief operating officer. In March 2003, Maguire stepped down as CEO. Graves replaced him, promising to make developing "a constant stream of new products" the centerpiece of a new company strategy.[22] Establishing an Innovation Center at the company's headquarters in South Carolina, KEMET introduced the AO-CAP, a solid aluminum capacitor, and the KO-MAT, the world's fastest tantalum capacitor, designed to improve power management in high frequency electronics such as notebooks, video game systems, and high end computer servers.

Perhaps the most important initiative under Graves's tenure was the establishment of a new plant in Suzhou, China, which began production in late 2003 and within a year was shipping more than 10 billion units. Like Matamoros and other Mexican border cities in the late 1960s, Suzhou emerged in the mid 1990s as a vital production center catering to a global industry. Located near the

KEMET personnel in Suzhou, China, produce billions of tantalum capacitors each year.

Shanghai financial hub and drawing on a highly skilled labor pool, the Suzhou industrial park today occupies an area of nearly 300 square kilometers. Some 25,000 companies maintain facilities in Suzhou, including a great many of KEMET's most important customers. One of Maguire's principle tenets as president was that the company should be "easy to buy from." Establishing a factory in China and growing its sales force in the region extended that value to its growing base of customers in Asia. In June 2004, KEMET began construction on a second facility in Suzhou, which would open in March 2005. "These operations represent a cornerstone of our strategy to have a distinctive, seamless system of global demand fulfillment," Graves said.[23]

Unfortunately, the force of the fallout from the dot-com bubble overwhelmed these savvy management decisions. KEMET and its competitors continued to struggle to stay afloat. Telecommunications giants Cisco and Qualcomm teetered on the brink of collapse, while many other communications firms and online shopping sites that once seemed so promising failed altogether. One of the most famous examples being Pets.com, which one business analyst has described as "one of the shortest-lived public companies on record."[24] Pets.com was founded in

When the "irrational exuberance" surrounding technology stocks crashed in March 2001, it took years for the electronics industry to recover.

November 1998, raised $82.5 million at its initial public offering on Nasdaq in February 2000, and went into liquidation in November 2000. A series of accounting scandals in the early 2000s — Enron, Worldcom, Adelphia, and Arthur Anderson — made things even worse. On October 4, 2002, the Nasdaq-100 hit its nadir, falling to just over 1100 points, a staggering loss of 78 percent against its March 2000 peak of over 5000 points.

In this bleak climate, KEMET may have struggled, but it never floundered. About half of the company's income came from distributors who supplied the general market. With so many anticipated customers going out of business, inventory at the distributors piled up, and KEMET's sales to manufacturers of computers, business equipment, and telecommunications equipment flattened. What kept the company going were the specialty products and high reliability materials KEMET produced for other sectors, including the automotive industry, industrial equipment, and defense and aerospace applications. The latter category, which included avionics, radar, guidance systems, and satellite communications, accounted for less than three percent of net sales during fiscal year 2004.[25]

Facing mounting losses — $112 million in 2004 and $174 million in 2005 — Graves resigned in January 2005. In March, David Maguire retired as chairman of the board after 43 years with KEMET. In April, 2005 the board brought in a new CEO, Per-Olof Loof, an executive with extensive experience in company management. Educated at the Stockholm School of Economics, Loof brought to KEMET lessons learned working with Anderson Consulting, Digital, AT&T, NCR, and Sensormatic Electronics, as well as the QuanStar Group, a management consulting firm. "KEMET's mission is to return to profitability as soon as possible," he announced. "The math must work."[26]

Loof initiated a number of changes at KEMET. First, he rebranded the company from the inside out. Developing a visionary platform known as "The Themes Document," the company replaced the five core values that had been in place since the 1980s with five new themes, and defined eight new priorities. "Now it's time for the next stage in our evolution — from being a capacitor supplier to *The Capacitance Company*," Loof wrote. KEMET "is to be the first company any electronics company calls for anything in this category, from products to design collaboration to custom development."[27] The company adopted a new motto, "Charged," which Loof noted, "accurately reflects our leadership teams, our reinvigorated sales and engineering groups, and the attitude of the entire company."[28]

KEMET also affirmed its commitment to research, releasing 1,000 new products in the fiscal year ending March 2006, 114 of which were first-to-market in the industry. In fiscal year 2007, the company introduced 4,070 new products, of which 450 were first-to-market. The engine of this reinvigorated approach to innovation at KEMET was the newly established Advanced Technology Group led by Dr. Philip Lessner. Educated at Cooper Union and the University of California at Berkeley, Lessner joined KEMET in 1996 to work on tantalum projects. Ten years later he was named chief technology officer. Under his guidance, the Advanced Technology Group continues to create new state-of-the-art products, evaluate alliance and acquisition projects, and establish relationships with educational and research institutions.

In addition to filing new patents, the company furthered its progress in becoming a truly global enterprise by opening a second factory in China and brokering a cooperative alliance with a Japanese company, Taiyo Yuden. Finally in April 2006, KEMET acquired the tantalum capacitor business EPCOS AG, which included a manufacturing operation in Evora, Portugal, and facilities in Germany. This latter move would mark an important shift in KEMET's business strategy, where the innovation and invention that had always characterized the company's approach would be supplemented by mergers and acquisitions. In 2007, KEMET made two other acquisitions to expand its offerings in aluminum electrolytic and film capacitors. Evox Rifa Group, based in Finland, and Arcotronics, an Italian company. With these purchases came 13 manufacturing plants in Bulgaria, China, Finland, Germany, Italy, Sweden, and the United Kingdom. These acquisitions offered KEMET a vital foothold in the European market.

Thus reinvigorated, the company turned a very modest profit in fiscal year 2006, its first year in the black since 2002. Fiscal year 2007 was even better, but then things turned down again. Here too, larger economic factors were to blame. A collapse in the subprime mortgage market in the United States led to the ruin of Lehman Brothers and other investment banks, culminating in a full-scale global financial crisis. Among the many sectors affected were the automotive and

continued on page 124

KEMET'S THEMES

- **THE MATH MUST WORK!**
- **HEAR THE CUSTOMERS AND BE RESPONSIVE.**
- **LIGHT THE FIRE! SHOW YOU CARE!**
- **BUILD WHAT THE CUSTOMER WANTS.**
- **BECOME THE CAPACITANCE COMPANY.**

KEMET'S PRIORITIES

FLATTEN THE ORGANIZATION
Create a business unit and regional structure, and continue to build the organization for the next level.

TECHNOLOGY
Be a leader — develop what the customer wants — focus on speed to market, and do it right the first time.

QUALITY AND RELIABILITY
Must be a given in the minds of our customers.

SHORT WIP — ONE ROOF STRATEGY
Build the product, from beginning to end, under one roof.

LOW-COST LOCATIONS
Produce our products in low-cost locations and close to the customer.

THE PEOPLE AT THE FRONT LINE CALL THE SHOTS
Corporate's role is to support the business units and the regional units.

BRAND KEMET
Capitalize on our excellent reputation.

EASY-TO-BUY-FROM (ETBF)
Focus on customer service in everything we do — remain the ETBF industry leader.

Personnel at KEMET in Mexico formed a running team in 2015 to build camaraderie and support healthy lifestyles.

Personnel at KEMET's offices in Simpsonville, SC, gather to celebrate International Women's Day, 2019.

KEMET's distribution team coordinates the worldwide delivery of billions of components each year.

KEMET personnel in Ciudad Victoria, Mexico, are recognized for the consistent high quality of their products.

THE KISENGO FOUNDATION

Tantalum, the primary ingredient of KEMET's signature product, has always been a troublesome element. A rare mineral occurring always in conjunction with niobium, another rare element, tantalum was discovered in 1802. It took over 125 years to develop an efficient process for separating the two metals. The name of the element reflects the frustration scientists felt with working with it: tantalum is named after Tantalus, a Greek mythological figure who was condemned to stand in water that he could not drink and beneath ripe fruit that he could not reach.

KEMET's investment in a tantalum mining operation in the Democratic Republic of Congo ensured that its supply chain was vertically integrated and ethically sourced.

KISENGO FOUNDATION

Coltan — the ore that contains tantalum and niobium — is mined in only a few parts of the world. In the 1950s and 1960s, the vast majority came from Nigeria, which at the time produced four-fifths of the global supply of tantalum.[29] Over the years, other major sources of tantalum have included Canada, Brazil, Australia, Mozambique, China, Rwanda, and the Democratic Republic of Congo (DRC). But the ethics of extraction could be extremely complicated — local competition for coltan reserves was one of the factors that sustained a long running civil war in the DRC. Unsafe working conditions and child labor also tainted much of the tantalum supply. Because such minerals are typically sold through brokers, it can be impossible to determine their exact origins.

So in 2011, KEMET took extraordinary measures to ensure that its tantalum was ethically sourced. Partnering with two mineral companies, the company acquired an interest in a tantalum mine in the DRC's Katanga Province to produce conflict-free ore. In February 2012, KEMET acquired a processing facility to serve the mine, and in August 2012 the company produced its first batch of guaranteed conflict-free capacitors.

KEMET's Kisengo Foundation supports schools, clinics, and other facilities needed by the residents of Katanga Province.

Simultaneously, KEMET and its partners established the Kisengo Foundation, a philanthropic venture designed to improve conditions for everyone in the region. Among the Foundation's major projects were a new school that by 2015 had provided education and vocational training to more than 1,800 students, and a hospital that had treated over 900 patients, in addition to a range of infrastructural improvements including wells, solar powered streetlights, and new roads and bridges. As then-CEO Per Olof Loof noted, "We believe the KEMET partnership can serve as a blueprint for responsible companies worldwide and demonstrate that solutions combining social sustainability and economic interests are not mutually exclusive."[30]

electronics industries, which experienced steep declines in sales. As unemployment climbed to a level not seen since the Great Depression, the stock market tumbled. On October 8, 2008, KEMET's stock dipped below one dollar per share and continued to decline in the months that followed. By January 2009, KEMET's finances had sunk so low that the company was removed from the NYSE. KEMET was once again compelled to take emergency measures. It closed its facility in Fountain Inn, SC. It reduced its global workforce by 20 percent and cut salaries by 10 percent. To avoid going into default on its debt, the company sold its wet tantalum capacitor product line, which included assets purchased from Arcotronics the year before, refinanced a €50 million loan due in December 2008 with a €60 million loan due April 2013, and negotiated a tender offer for the repurchase and retirement of a significant portion of its corporate debt.[31]

In today's world you need to be honest and clear with your people.

– CEO Per-Olof Loof on corporate communications

Loof and his team introduced one other significant change to help the company through this difficult time, and this was purely internal. The KEMET of the past had an exceptional esprit de corps built through company wide picnics, newsletters, and social events. Company employees of the 1980s and 1990s commonly likened themselves to members of an extended family. A number of employees had even found spouses among their coworkers. But that was when the company was concentrated in one small region of South Carolina. How was KEMET to maintain that extraordinary spirit now that it was global?

Loof's solution was technological. Using what was then cutting edge technology, he introduced company wide town hall meetings through teleconferencing. Four times a year, he spoke before several hundred employees representing different segments of the company. The event was broadcast to KEMET locations worldwide, and translated into multiple languages. In the early days of webcasting, these events were enormous undertakings costing more than $100,000 each time. But Loof insisted that it was worth it. "In today's world you need to be honest and clear with your people," he said. "It can't just be corporate da-da-da stuff."[32] The company continues to use webinars and intensive seminars to ensure that staff across the globe have the same access to executive communications, best practices, and technological developments.

These savvy management decisions ultimately reduced KEMET's debt by approximately $47 million, and provided the liquidity needed for the company to move forward on solid footing. By 2010, the worst of the recession was over and the market was back on its feet. The electronics industry had gone through a hard time, with many smaller components companies going under. KEMET had not only survived, but emerged stronger than ever and poised for growth. KEMET returned to the NYSE in November 2010 at $14 per share, and closed out the 2011 fiscal year with revenues in excess of $1 billion. Restored financially, KEMET resumed its path of global growth. In 2011, the company acquired Cornell Dubilier Foil, a Tennessee-based manufacturer of etched and formed aluminum foils, essential components of aluminum electrolytic capacitors, and redoubled its efforts in both film and electrolytic capacitors as well as high voltage and high capacitance organic polymer products. The following year, KEMET would finally address its tantalum problem head on.

A rare earth metal, tantalum is the central ingredient of KEMET's signature product. But throughout the company's history of producing capacitors, KEMET had been at the mercy of a market that fluctuated wildly and unpredictably. In 2000, for example, the price of tantalum averaged about $50 per pound. A year later, it shot up to $300 a pound. Given the quantities KEMET regularly consumed for its products, even smaller differentials — $175 in 2008, $194 in 2009 — made a significant impact for a company bent on rational financial planning. In 2001, KEMET entered into a joint venture with an Australian mining firm in an effort to stabilize its source of raw materials. In 2012, it went even further, acquiring a tantalum processing plant in Carson City, NV, which it subsequently renamed KEMET Blue Powder. The same year, KEMET entered into an exclusive arrangement with a South African mining company to mine tantalum ore from Katanga Province in the DRC. With this latter contract, KEMET not only stabilized its supply chain, it also took measures to ensure that its stock of this precious resource would be ethically sourced. By establishing the Kisengo Foundation, KEMET became the world's largest vertically integrated manufacturer of conflict-free capacitors and the world's largest user of capacitor-grade tantalum powder. At the same time, the company established its commitment to the duties of responsible global citizenship.

In the years since, KEMET has continued to expand. In fiscal year 2013, the company built a new chemical plant in Matamoros to produce potassium heptafluorotantalate (better known as K-salt), a key material in the processing of tantalum ore into powder. In addition to new products released each year, KEMET has designed custom solutions through its collaborative engineering services. For one such project, KEMET developed a multilayer ceramic capacitor that could perform in harsh subterranean oil and gas drilling environments. Other custom development projects focused on car headlight systems, tantalum stacks designed to reduce hard disk failure, DC link capacitors (for use in alternative energy applications including solar, wind, and hybrid and electric vehicles), and materials for cutting edge medical innovations such as neuro-modulation and sensory implants for vision and hearing. Through the KEMET Institute of Techno ogy (KIT), the company offers seminars and workshops to thousands of engineers, designers, and decision makers each year, around the world.

On April 19, 2017, KEMET completed its most important acquisition to date, purchasing TOKIN from the Japanese conglomerate NEC. Begun as a joint venture in 2012, this deal vastly expanded KEMET's product portfolio, which would now include inductors, sensors, actuators, and electromagnetic interference (EMI) suppression devices used to harness renewable energy. The deal also significantly increased KEMET's footprint in Asia, opening wide the vital Japanese marketplace in electronics.

The acquisition of TOKIN capped a decade of mergers and acquisitions that has positioned KEMET as a leading supplier of essential electronic components worldwide. In December 2018, the board elected a new CEO and Director, William M. Lowe, Jr., who had joined the company ten years earlier to serve as executive vice president and chief financial officer. KEMET's remarkable growth from a small lab in Cleveland to a global powerhouse with more than 20 facilities located in 18 countries on four continents captures in microcosm the story of American innovation over the 20th century and beyond. If history is any judge, KEMET's next 100 years will be just as exciting.

TOKIN

TOKIN, which has been manufacturing capacitors since 1958, has always been a worldwide leader in electronic components and material science. The company was founded in 1938 as Tohoku Metal Industries Co., Ltd., by Hakaru Masumoto and Tatsuji Yamamoto, two scientists at Tohoku University seeking to develop innovative magnetic technologies. In 1956, they began to produce ferrite cores used for electrical transformers and other wound components. In 1960, the company introduced its first solid tantalum capacitor, revolutionizing the Japanese electronics industry in the process.

Tohoku Metal Industries changed its name to TOKIN in 1983. That same year it opened its first overseas plant in Thailand; additional facilities in China and Vietnam would follow. In 2002, TOKIN merged with the electronic components division of the NEC Corporation, a venerable Japanese company founded in 1899 in association with the U.S. firm Western Electric. KEMET acquired the combined company, NEC-Tokin, in 2018.

For decades, TOKIN and its predecessors have been the principal suppliers of capacitors and other electronic devices to much of Asia. Among TOKIN's most high profile projects is its development of a circuit featuring a samarium-cobalt magnet for the Hayabusa2, an unmanned space vehicle that in 2019 collected samples from the asteroid Ryugu before returning to earth.

In addition to capacitors, TOKIN manufactures multilayer piezoelectric sensors and actuators, Flex Suppressors, electromagnets, inductors, noise filters, and alloys including Memoalloy, a highly flexible nickel-titanium blend used for surgical applications. With this acquisition, KEMET entered into a major new phase in its development as a leading manufacturer of electronic components. **K**

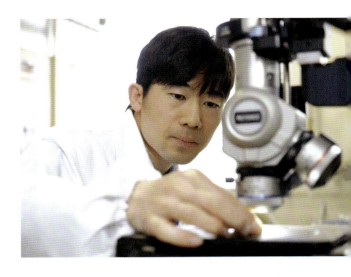

For decades, TOKIN's scientists have defined the cutting edge of electronics research in Japan.

KEMET's acquisition of TOKIN inaugurates a major new stage of growth for the company. Left to right: Per-Olof Loof (KEMET), Yasuko Matsumoto (NEC), Shigenori Oyama (TOKIN).

CHAPTER FIVE:

BUILT INTO TOMORROW

THE FUTURE OF INNOVATION AT KEMET IS ELECTRIFYING. WHILE THERE IS NO TELLING precisely what it will bring, one thing is certain: KEMET employees will continue to dedicate themselves to solving the world's most pressing scientific and environmental challenges, while KEMET products and solutions will power the technologies and industries of tomorrow. Today, KEMET is one of the world's most trusted partners for innovative component solutions. Looking ahead, the company will remain committed to making the world a better, safer, more connected place to live.

From Hugh S. Cooper's time to the present, KEMET has had a 100-year long track record of research on the cutting edge. Sometimes the company has acted as a fast follower, licensing the inventions of other organizations to bring them early to market. This was the case with KEMET's first line of capacitors in the late 1950s. At other times, the company has collaborated with manufacturers and made important breakthroughs in technology to produce custom products. This was the case with high performance conductive polymer tantalum capacitors in 1998, which KEMET developed jointly with the NEC Corporation under their respective product names, KO-CAPs® (KEMET) and NeoCapacitors™ (NEC). But KEMET is most celebrated for its history of invention. The company has secured hundreds of patents, and over the years

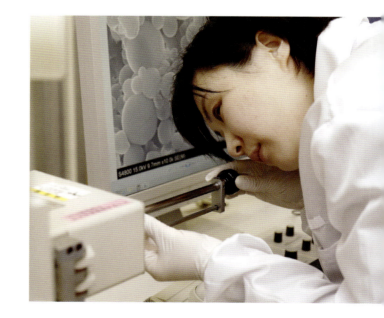

KEMET's continuous investment in innovation has made the company a leader in the industry.

KEMET HAS A 100-YEAR LONG TRACK RECORD
OF RESEARCH ON THE CUTTING EDGE

its acquisitions have added hundreds more to its portfol o. Today, KEMET controls 313 patents in the United States and 1,006 internationally.[1]

Because KEMET is a technology company, simply keeping abreast of the current state of science is not enough. Innovation in the electronics marketplace moves so quickly that any company that lingers too long behind the curve will find itself antiquated. Investing hundreds of millions of dollars in the 1980s and 1990s to expand its manufacturing facilities from leaded capacitors to surface-mount devices was an incredibly risky move at a time when the future of that technology was so uncertain. KEMET's boldness allowed it to maintain its position at the top while less venturesome companies watched their market

John Piper (right), with Gordon Love. Piper guided scientific research at KEMET for almost three decades after his arrival in South Carolina in 1967.

shares dwindle. Every year, the company invests tens of millions of dollars on research and development — almost $40 million in fiscal year 2018.[2]

KEMET's first patents for solid tantalum capacitors were filed in 1963. They included processes for producing tantalum capacitors, and a process for screening them for reliability.[3] The latter represented a fundamental breakthrough, not only for KEMET but also for the industry as a whole.[4] Today KEMET's process is still used to establish the reliability of space- and defense-grade components. KEMET scientists were responsible for one of the company's most important inventions of the 1970s, the hermetically-sealed solid electrolytic capacitor, which is still used in high reliability applications for defense and space.[5] KEMET's T110 series is a product of this technology, as is the T550/T551 series, based on KO-CAP® polymer technology.

Today, KEMET centers its research and development in multiple Innovation Centers in the United States, Japan, Italy, and Portugal. The entire program is organized through the Advanced Technology Group (ATG), which collaborates with academic institutions on research into fundamental issues in passive electronic components. The ATG is fundamental to what Chief Technology Officer Philip Lessner has called "the process of invention and reinvention" that has enabled the company to thrive at the cutting edge of scientific development.[6]

For much of the twentieth century, KEMET's signature product was a tantalum capacitor with a cathode composed of manganese dioxide (MnO_2). Beginning in the late 1990s, KEMET began transforming the technology by using intrinsically conductive polymers for the dielectric instead. The base technology came from NEC-TOKIN, but KEMET built it out with new processes developed in its South Carolina laboratories.[7]

KEMET's tantalum R&D in the late 1990s. Back row (left to right): Erwin Fischler, Phil Lessner, Brian Melody. Front row: Pete Orthman, Jim Marshall, Erik Reed.

Philip Lessner (front row, center), sitting with a few of his colleagues in China, coordinates KEMET's international program in research and development.

Ceramics is another field where KEMET has been leading the industry into exciting new directions. Today, the company has a robust ceramic capacitors program thanks largely to the skillful management during very difficult times. Ceramic capacitors had started out as a lucrative division for KEMET, but by the 1980s and 1990s, competition from Asian manufacturers had glutted the market, and prices were steadily dropping. KEMET, facing a race to the bottom, was losing money each year. The financial stresses of the 2000s dot-com bubble burst made continuing along such uncertain lines untenable, so managers at KEMET redefined the program, eliminating the common products that were losing money to focus on specialty ceramics, in particular dielectrics for high temperature, high voltage, and high power applications.[8] Today, KEMET leads the field in the technology of Class I ceramic dielectrics that are used in applications where extreme voltage and temperature stability are needed. These applications include new power conversion technologies and operation in harsh and demanding environments such as down hole drilling.

The fundamental materials patent for KEMET's Class I dielectrics, filed in 2005, substituted nickel for palladium and silver as the electrode material.[9] This led to a series of base metal electrode (BME) ceramics that were not only much less expensive than earlier generations of ceramic capacitors

KEMET's scientists have made major breakthroughs in reinventing tantalum capacitors for the 21st century.

but also higher performing. KEMET's explorations in ceramic materials today are exemplified by such inventions as the KC-LINK™ capacitor, a device designed for use in fast switching, wide bandgap semiconductor applications, increasingly important in automotive electronics. KEMET's ceramics team also customizes materials for BME high reliability components used in demanding defense and aerospace applications.

KEMET's products in the fields of film and aluminum electrolytic capacitors are used in solar converters, wind generators, trains, hybrid vehicles, power supplies, and other crucial automotive and industrial applications. Other new products include the ArcShield™, which uses a special electrode design to produce the smallest high volate capacitors on the market. KEMET KONNEKT™ is a novel way of connecting capacitors though an innovative transient liquid phase sintering (TLPS) technology that binds component terminals together. KEMET is also developing an electrostatic discharge (ESD) suppressor that has the potential to offer new levels of protection for electronic circuits. The most recent frontier is comprised of modules that integrate multiple components through a common terminal. A single module might be comprised of multiple capacitors, or of a capacitor combined with inductors to serve as a Pi filter. This approach increases functionality while reducing the space that would be required were the components placed separately.

INNOVATION AT TOKIN

KEMET's acquisition of TOKIN brought to the company a host of important and innovative products that will serve as the fundamental components of our technological future. Even more importantly, this brought KEMET a number of brilliant researchers in materials science whose work has continued to define the cutting edge.

TOKIN's history of innovation began with the work of its founders on ferrite cores and electromagnets (see page 127). The company invented the first noise suppression sheet, introduced in 1995. Marketed under the name Flex Suppressor™, the invention absorbs high frequency noise and other undesirable waves generated by electrical devices and converts them into heat to create a clean electromagnetic environment. The suppressor is composed of overlapping ultra thin magnetic metal foils, each only a few microns thick. For this and later developments, TOKIN scientists were awarded the Contribution Prize of the Ichimura Prizes in Industry in 2008.

KEMET maintains Innovation Centers throughout Japan. In Sendai, scientists conduct research on materials development. In Shiroishi, they focus on magnetic and piezoelectric products. In Toyama, a team focusing on tantalum coordinates their research with colleagues in the United States. Satellite plants for magnetic and piezoelectric projects are located in Vietnam and Xiamen, China.

Over the years, these scientists and their colleagues have been responsible for a remarkable array of extraordinary inventions. These include SENNTIX™, a metallic glass dust powder used to improve efficiency in power supply systems. A choke coil using this material won the 57th Electrical Science and Engineering Promotion Award in 2009. In 2011, researchers at the company invented a highly sensitive surface-mount pyroelectric infrared sensor. In 2012, they developed a piezoelectric acoustic receiver for smartphones. Other major inventions in include S18H, a ferrite used for noise suppression, introduced in 2014, and Senfoliage™, a sheeted high flex density magnetic material used to minimize the size of DC/DC converters. **K**

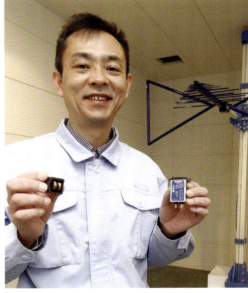

Top: Some of TOKIN's leading scientists visit facilities in South Carolina.

Bottom: Koki Harada, senior manager for magnetic product engineering, stands in an anechoic chamber, with two of KEMET's products, an AC line filter and a noise filter.

KEMET's expansion over the past decade has brought the company a rich array of products that will serve as the building blocks for our technological future. Like capacitors, KEMET's new products are classified as "passive components," electrical devices that (unlike "active components") do not need power in order to operate. The first step in this direction was in 1997, when KEMET formed a technical partnership with Taiyo Yuden, a leading Japanese components manufacturer. In 2006, this partnership blossomed into a formal strategic alliance that allowed the companies to market each other's products. Through further research and expansion, KEMET's amazing array of products now includes such items as:

PYROELECTRIC SENSORS

Compact sensors that control and adjust devices when they detect heat and human motion, resulting in energy savings and improved convenience. Inconspicuous, low profile, and requiring no lens, they are unobtrusively incorporated into a wide range of products.

VIBRATION SENSORS

Highly sensitive piezoelectric sensors that can be used to determine the operational status of equipment. Simplifying diagnostics and preventative maintenance, they support the progress of "the Internet of Things (IoT)" in smart factories.

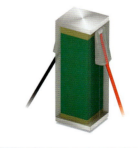

MULTILAYER PIEZOELECTRIC ACTUATORS

Ceramic devices converting electrical energy in precisely controlled physical displacements (or "strokes"). These are used for the sort of delicate motion control required for nanotechnology-based equipment that relies on precise positioning.

PIEZO RECEIVERS / SPEAKERS

These acoustic modules generate sound through the vibration of a piezoelectric element that may be placed on a device's surface. The design flexibility improves acoustics and renders standard audio elements (such as a hole in the product body) unnecessary. Currently used in smartphones, they are expected to have a wide range of applications in the future.

CHOKE COILS

Filters that improve noise suppression effects in a range of home appliances and electronics, from air conditioners to 8K ultra high resolution televisions. KEMET produces these in a range of sizes and configurations.

SUPER CAPACITORS

Double layer, high capacity devices that have proven reliability during prolonged use in severe conditions. They are used for robots, smart meters, medical devices, and industrial systems.

FLEX SUPPRESSOR

A material that absorbs the noise radiated from electronic devices, improving reception sensitivity, and decreasing internal interference. Produced as sheets, Flex Suppressor can simply be attached to the motherboards of PCs and smartphones in the final stages of assembly.

METAL COMPOSITE INDUCTORS

Vital components that store electrical energy in the form of magnetic energy. They are popularly used to support extended battery life at low consumption in automobiles, laptops and other devices that must operate long hours between charges.

CURRENT SENSORS

Relying on patented magnetic alloys, these highly sensitive devices are used for monitoring power conditioners and home energy management systems (HEMS).

HEAT RESISTANT SmCo MAGNETS

Composed of a samarium-cobalt (SmCo) alloy, these magnets have superior heat resistance that realize better results than conventional magnets. They are used for harsh, high temperature environments such as car motors.

METAL COMPOSITE REACTORS

Integrally molded using KEMET's unique technology, the metal composite reactor optimizes the performance of boost inverters in hybrid vehicles.

KEMET scientist Yuri Freeman receives the Ekeberg Prize for his contributions to the study of tantalum and niobium capacitors.

Materials scientists at KEMET develop new compounds to improve component performance.

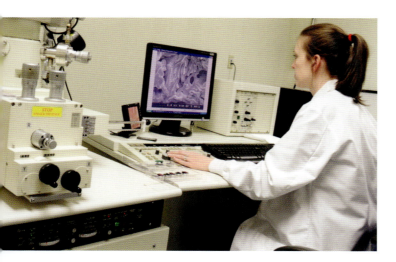

In 2010, KEMET's then-CEO Per-Olof Loof wrote about the ways the company's products are embedded in our everyday lives:

> *"The next time you drive your car to take that someone special out on the town, take an airplane flight with your family on vacation, turn on your computer to send an e-mail to mom, read a story about a new space mission or new alternative energy technologies, or see the look on a loved one's face who has been given a second chance on life due to a breakthrough medical device — know that you're likely to find a piece of KEMET technology in these products. No, capacitors are not the most glamorous devices in the world of technology — but the world stops without them."*[10]

Those words ring even more soundly today, thanks to the company's expanded line of products. The basic but extraordinarily sophisticated components and technologies manufactured by KEMET permeate every aspect of our daily lives. They are found in the lighting that illuminates our homes, the televisions and consoles that provide interactive entertainment, and the sensor systems that keep our families safe and comfortable. They are responsible for energy efficiency, reliability and safety of digital devices, and industrial equipment. And they fuel the devices that drive our networked society, from computers to smartphones to tablets and other equipment that allow us to communicate with each other and control devices from virtually anywhere in the world.

Engineers develop new applications for KEMET products.

KEMET is building the future, component by component. The company sells billions of its products each year. It has also built on its long tradition of producing customized products tailored to the unique requirements of individual clients and specialized applications. KEMET's application engineers collaborate with customer design engineers to build out new products and think through solutions in bold, creative ways. KEMET also collaborates with professors on three continents to bring the full force of new academic research to product development. TOKIN has a long established relationship with the world class scholars at Tohuku University in Japan. In South Carolina, KEMET researchers collaborate with faculty at Clemson University on electron microscopy to add new analysis techniques. "We can now do surface depth profiling, for example," notes one of the company's leading scientists, "which is helpful in understanding very thin coatings used in biomedical, automotive, aerospace, and many other applications."[11]

In 2019, the company launched the KEMET Application Intelligence Center (KAIC), an innovation lab located at the company's global headquarters in Fort Lauderdale, FL. The Center focuses on exploring new applications, optimizing designs, and innovating with new solutions. KAIC serves as an educational lab for students and professionals alike.

The Hayabusa2 space probe relied on components from TOKIN.

As the director explains, "The lab has three main audiences: people who are just getting into electronics, budding engineers, and also seasoned engineers who are incorporating detailed concepts. KAIC is the place to explore application design with KEMET."[12]

The new directions made possible by KEMET's products and technologies are almost limitless. The knowledge base of the electronics industry grows exponentially each year, and new tools, techniques, and applications are developed every day. KEMET's components are optimized not only for the work that is being done today, but also for the ideas that are being engineered for tomorrow.

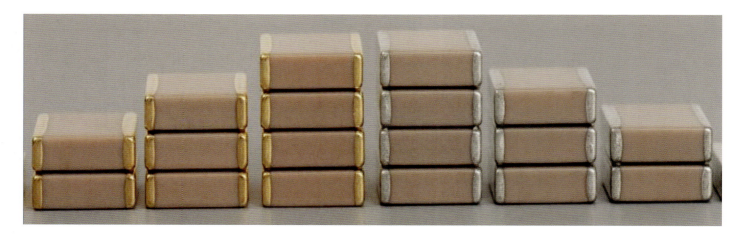

KEMET's most recent line of high performance ceramic capacitors can be stacked to maximize efficiency. They were designed for high power density converter applications such as solar arrays, wind turbines, electric vehicles, and data centers.

One of the most exciting new developments involves high power delivery networks, which charge electronic devices wirelessly, from mobile phones to electric vehicles. Imagine being able to charge your phone while it is in your pocket, or having your electric car charged as you drive. This sounds like the stuff of science fiction, but these inventions are available now as prototypes. Soon they will be widespread, and powered by components from KEMET.

The Internet of Things (IoT) revolution, which allows for the instantaneous transfer of data across multiple platforms, has already begun to transform every aspect of peoples' lives. The new generation of wireless connectivity is characterized by instant downloads, immersive gaming, and

KEMET's Film Innovation Center and manufacturing facility in Pontecchio, Italy, opened in 2013.

The Electrolytic Innovation Center in Evora, Portugal, develops new materials for autonomous vehicles and other applications.

more efficient communications. Just as KEMET helped to power innovations that shaped the last information age, so too will KEMET components be central to these new developments, enabling connectivity and protecting data by providing continual power management in the cloud.

The IoT revolution has implications for transportation. Since the 1950s, KEMET has had relationships with nearly every major automaker, providing components such as capacitors for automotive electronics systems as well as products for automotive safety and control systems. KEMET components are embedded in virtually every corner of the modern automobile: the company's products provide the essential building blocks for safety systems including anti-lock brakes, airbags, steering control, crash avoidance systems, backup cameras, and adaptive headlights. KEMET components power dashboard, navigation, and entertainment systems, and ensure the reliable operation of the batteries, fuel pumps, speed sensors, traction controls, and power trains that keep cars running.

KEMET's products will continue to be essential even as IoT, edge computing, autonomous vehicles, and advanced driver assistance systems (ADAS) stand to upend the automotive industry as we know it. Historically, car companies have tended to focus on their research and development efforts on core aspects of the vehicle, such as the engine and body design. Other aspects of the car, including its electronics systems, were typically handled by third party suppliers, which KEMET supported with components specifically designed for automotive applications.

Autonomous vehicles equipped with sensory technologies will be only one feature of our dawning new world. The IoT revolution is also transforming our urban environments. Indeed, the emergence of the fully realized "smart city" is already visible in a wide range of recent urban planning initiatives. Barcelona has installed a fiber-optic network providing the public with free internet access and enabling the integration of the city's public utilities and parking management systems. Seattle has installed smart traffic lights capable of responding to the ebb and flow of daily commutes. Milton Keynes, England, features a hub allowing for the real-time monitoring of the city's energy use, water consumption, and weather patterns.

The KEMET Application Intelligence Center serves as a space for young engineers and seasoned veterans to explore new uses for KEMET's cutting edge technology.

A smart city built on a network of sensors will be able to regulate traffic, lighting, utilities, and other services to reduce resource consumption and waste. With these systems in place, for instance, automobile camera and sensor data could be used to monitor roads for traffic, potholes, or other adverse driving conditions. Then, leveraging this data, monitoring services could alert cars in near real time to traffic accidents, simultaneously adjusting travel routes to optimized detours while dispatching emergency vehicles. Unlike applications already used by drivers, the vehicle itself would select a new route based on the data shared by the monitoring system — all to ease traffic and improve safety.

No less than the city, the home is one of the great frontiers of the IoT revolution. Smart building systems — including individual homes — increasingly rely on connected devices to perform small tasks that have a big impact, whether it is raising the heat when the temperature falls or lowering the blinds when the sun is bright. In the future, smart homes will ensure that our pantries are stocked with food and that we never run out of the medicine on which we depend.

KEMET is building materials for the information and communication infrastructure required to bring the urban and domestic futures envisioned by the IoT revolution to fruition. KEMET's components are designed for the powerful new networks and hyperscale data centers that can recognize patterns and generate appropriate responses instantaneously. The future will harness the connective potential of edge servers to bring network power ever closer and smaller. KEMET is working on materials designed to maximize efficiency in the power topologies of the switched tank converters (STCs) that are being built to accommodate the data processing needs of the future.

In the field of healthcare, KEMET has built on its history of designing materials for pacemakers and defibrillators by aiding the unfolding revolution in medical electronics. These range from improved large scale diagnostic tools such as computerized tomography to microscopic machines, such as nanorobots, which are capable of delivering drugs, reconstructing bones, treating cancer, addressing blood clots, removing kidney stones, and performing other intelligent tasks at the nanoscale.

KEMET's piezoelectric polymers are being developed as haptic actuators for gaming devices, medical devices, and other applications, extending our sense of touch. With currently available technology, haptic devices — such as smartphones and virtual reality (VR) gloves — vibrate. KEMET's new technology will change that, providing meaningful and highly localized feedback by controlling the wave shape, duty cycle, amplitude, and frequency of pulses. Imagine VR gloves in which one feels the rain not as a vibration in the hand, but as individual raindrops hitting the skin. KEMET and its collaborators are making that a reality.

KEMET makes components of exquisite sensitivity, but they make rugged parts too. In fact, KEMET's history of producing high reliability components is particularly important with the IoT revolution. The communications and data platforms that will define the future require a broad range of electronics components, including semiconductors, magnetics, capacitors, actuators, and sensors. Some of these will be in accessible facilities, but many others will be situated in remote locations with limited access to traditional power sources. They will need to be able to operate at

KEMET components are powering the new frontier in electric and autonomcus vehicles.

very low levels of power, or even to harvest their own energy in harsh, all-weather conditions. The components that KEMET developed to be resistant to heat, humidity, rain and thermal shock, will be critical.

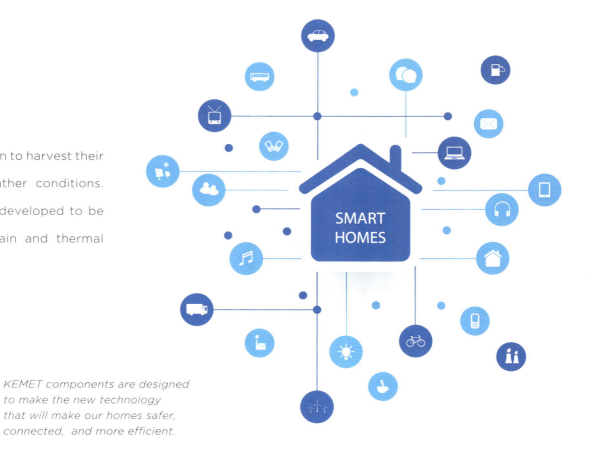

KEMET components are designed to make the new technology that will make our homes safer, connected, and more efficient.

Sensors and other KEMET products will be integral to the smart cities of the future.

The high reliability components that KEMET first developed for Telstar and NASA will be in even more demand as the conquest of space becomes an ever nearing goal for both government agencies and private companies. KEMET continues to produce materials for use in the final frontier. Every product that KEMET designs for launchpads, reusable rockets, spacecrafts, and exploratory probes is designed to withstand extreme conditions of heat and cold. KEMET's long record of achievement, and the bonds of reliability that the company has established by working on secure projects, ensure that it will play a major role in future space missions to the moon, Mars, and beyond.

Closer to home, KEMET's high reliability components are vital to the alternative energy technologies that are responsible for building a greener, cleaner world. This includes not only large scale solutions such as harnessing wind, solar, geothermal, and tidal energy. It also includes microsolutions, such as improving the efficiency of energy transfer in data server systems. New designs created by KEMET now enable incremental improvements in efficiency that will have dramatic impacts across systems — on a global scale, reducing energy by even as little as 0.5 percent will significantly reduce carbon emissions. As the reach of cloud computing continues to accelerate, KEMET's components will create a future in which ambitious technology and sustainable energy consumption go hand in hand.

Piezoelectric polymers from KEMET are revolutionizing haptics, the technology that simulates the sensations of touch.

As a ccmpany dedicated to social and economic sustainability, KEMET has made environmental stewardship part of its own mission. The company was an early and active advocate for sustainability both in its direct operations and across its entire supply chain. Even as the company has continued its trend of dramatic growth around the world, its rigorous commitment to minimizing its environmental footprint has yielded impressive results. Between 2017 and 2018,

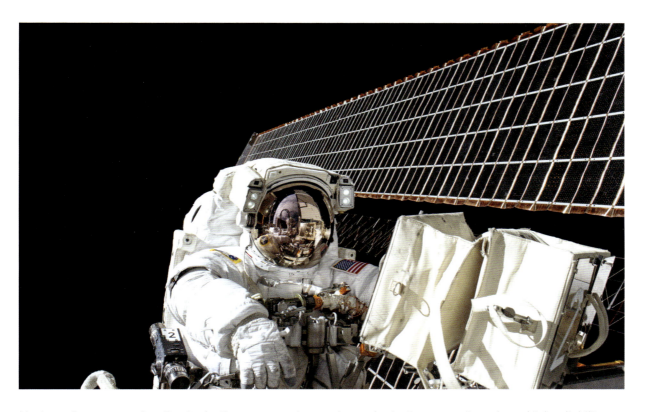

Ventures in space exploration by both government agencies and private companies rely on high reliability components from KEMET.

KEMET reduced its absolute carbon emissions from its direct operations by nearly 23 percent, vastly exceeding its stated goal of reductions of 3 percent per year. KEMET has also committed itself to conserving water supplies by instituting measures designed to minimize waste, ensuring strict compliance with local environmental laws. KEMET's facility located in Pontecchio, Italy, exemplif es the company's commitment to environmental sustainability practices. In 2018, the installation of new cooling systems there reduced water consumption by 50 percent, while a new trigeneration system has helped reduce carbon dioxide emissions by 50 percent — remarkable achievements that have raised the bar for sustainability across the company. As KEMET celebrates its 100th anniversary, this commitment to pursuing sustainable practices remains a top priority across the entire company. KEMET plans to tailor these efforts to the United Nations Sustainable Development Goals, thereby aligning the company with one of the world's leading standards of responsible global citizenship.

Perhaps no technology is as ambitious — or as hotly debated — as Artificial Intelligence (AI). Although achieving true sentience in a machine still lies far in the future, there have been many breakthroughs in a subfield known as Machine Learning (ML). Unlike the more general term AI, which refers to the simulation of intelligent behavior in machines, ML more specifically refers to computers that are trained to identify patterns across enormous data sets, often relating to specific tasks like image and voice recognition or translating text between languages. Given a complex question and a related data set, ML computers can infer the answer from a model developed during training. In more and more tasks, ML computers have surpassed even the most accomplished human practitioners.

For more than a generation, these breakthroughs in AI and ML have been based on and supported by the exponentially increasing processing power of computers and the availability of data itself. In particular, unstructured data, such as images, text, and video, have become a valuable resource to support the training of ML models. In addition to efficient data centers to support data collection, this development has also depended on power management at the scale of individual advanced processing computer chips. As it has done since the origins of the revolution in computer technology, KEMET has continued to develop capacitors that are cutting edge of materials and design.

KEMET's commitment to energy efficiency and environmental sustainability is central to its mission as a company.

One World. One KEMET.

There is one final way KEMET is working to build the components of the future. Ever since the 1930s, when the company's focus transitioned from research to production, KEMET has been proud of its diverse workforce. In 1946, when the company employed just 83 people, nearly half of them were women. This ratio stayed close to constant as the company embarked on a program of dramatic expansion in the decades that followed. As of 2018, KEMET's global workforce consisted of over 15,000 employees, of whom 54 percent were women. Reflecting its status as a truly global enterprise, KEMET's scientists and senior managers come from a wide range of backgrounds, representing China, Germany, Italy, Japan, Mexico, and the United States. Meanwhile, the

Future generations of scientists and entrepreneurs get their start through KEMET's high school internship programs.

company's 40 vice presidents represent fourteen countries of origin. Although the company is headquartered in the United States, its employees hail from all over the globe. This international perspective is what underlies the company's motto, "*One World. One KEMET.*"

KEMET is committed to supporting the diversity of future generations of scientists and engineers. To that end, the company has been a longtime contributor to programs such as Junior Achievement, the world's largest organization dedicated to inspiring and preparing young people to succeed in a global economy. KEMET provides funds, volunteers, and internship opportunities in support of the organization's core programs in work readiness, entrepreneurship, and financial literacy. Every year, high school students in South Carolina and Florida have the opportunity to work alongside KEMET's top researchers on dynamic projects. KEMET is also a proud supporter of For Inspiration and Recognition of Science and Technology (FIRST), which helps young people pursue careers in science, technology, engineering and mathematics (STEM) through educational and mentorship programs. Since the beginning of its relationship with FIRST, KEMET has supported nearly 850 teams participating in the organization's annual robotics competition, inspiring over 10,000 students in the process. The company's goal is to ensure that the diversity and inclusion that have long characterized KEMET are replicated across the entire field of STEM education.

For 100 years, KEMET has redefined the possibilities of electronics. From its humble beginnings in a modest laboratory, the company has evolved into a global powerhouse. Ever on the lookout for opportunities amidst periods of rapid change and formidable challenges, KEMET's people have set industry wide standards in quality. In the process of improving their products, the company has helped to shape the modern world. Thanks to the company's dedication to continuous research and innovation, and its mission to make the world a better, safer, more connected place to live, the KEMET of 2119 will surely be just as remarkable as the KEMET of today.

A NOTE ON NOMENCLATURE

Like people, companies change and adapt over time. They become bigger, more complex, and more sophisticated. They shift their focus, refine their business strategies, rearrange their operations. Some also change their names. And like individuals who might shed a childhood nickname to redefine themselves at adulthood, many companies rebrand themselves to mark a change in organization or mission. Also like adults who sometimes retain childhood nicknames, not all companies make clean breaks with earlier brands.

KEMET, for example, was founded (with lower case letters) as "Kemet Laboratories Company, Inc." During that early time period, the company principally served as a research arm of a much larger corporation, Union Carbide. KEMET focused on experiments in chemical metallurgy – the "chem" and "met" were fused together to create the name "Kemet." It was a tiny operation, occupying just one room. To capture the activity in this small space and the ambitions of its people, it included "Laboratories" to suggest a larger footprint. By 1933, KEMET had grown much bigger and shifted its focus to manufacturing. The company was no longer a research laboratory, and some publications started identifying it as the "Kemet Company," or the "Kemet Division" (of Union Carbide). But the old name stuck. In the late 1940s, the company identified itself as "Kemet Laboratories Company" on the containers of its principle product and as "The Kemet Company" in its trade catalogue. At this point, the company also adopted a logo with "KEMET" in capital letters that included a bar above and below the name (see the photograph of the getters can on page 53 of this book). KEMET was spelled using all capital letters and as "Kemet" interchangeably until the company went independent in 1987. And even then, the use of "Kemet" with lower case letters sometimes crept into company monikers. In this period, some of the company's longtime people appear to have forgotten, or disregarded, the policy of using all caps. In this book, our focus is the story, learnings, and accomplishments of KEMET. To avoid distracting the reader, we have chosen to use "KEMET" throughout, even when doing so may be interpreted as anachronistic.

Similarly, Union Carbide — KEMET's parent company until 1987 — also underwent many changes. Originating as the Union Carbide Company in 1890s, in 1917 it joined forces with four other companies to create the Union Carbide and Carbon Corporation, which is generally abbreviated as Union Carbide. This shorter name encompassed many smaller companies, including KEMET. In 1957, the corporation dropped "Carbon" from its name to become the Union Carbide Corporation, or, more simply, Union Carbide. Here, too, we use "Union Carbide" to refer to the corporation in its various manifestations.

Complicating this story further still, about ten years before Union Carbide formed KEMET it also acquired another company that is known as the Electro-Metallurgical Company (sometimes spelled without the hyphen), or, more familiarly, as Electromet. KEMET was under the supervision of the Electro-Metallurgical Company during its earliest years. Because of this, we have opted to retain the longer form of the company's name to maintain the sense of antiquity of what was once an important relationship during KEMET's formative years.

ENDNOTES

CHAPTER ONE

1 "United States Census, 1880," *FamilySearch*, Ohio > Cuyahoga > Cleveland > ED 29 > image 19 of 58; citing NARA microfilm publication T9, (National Archives and Records Administration, Washington, D.C., n.d.); "United States Census, 1900," *FamilySearch*, Ohio > Cuyahoga > ED 197 Precinct B Cleveland City Ward 40 > image 20 of 62; citing NARA microfilm publication T623 (Washington, D.C.: National Archives and Records Administration, n.d.); "United States Census, 1920," *FamilySearch*, John Cooper, Cleveland Ward 25, Cuyahoga, Ohio, United States; citing ED 483, sheet 7A, line 43, family 162, NARA microfilm publication T625 (Washington D.C.: National Archives and Records Administration, 1992), roll 1372; FHL microfilm 1,821,372.

2 Richard Klein, *The Legacy of the Pharmacy Industry: Cleveland, Ohio* (MSL Academic Endeavors eBooks, 2017) https://engagedscholarship.csuohio.edu/msl_ae_ebooks/5, p. 31; *Cleveland Plain Dealer*, June 18, 1907, p. 7; "United States Census, 1910," Hugh S. Cooper, Cleveland Ward 23, Cuyahoga, Ohio, United States; citing enumeration district (ED) ED 348, sheet 7A, family 151, NARA microfilm publication T624 (Washington D.C.: National Archives and Records Administration, 1982), roll 1175; FHL microfilm 1,375,188; *Cleveland City Directory for 1914-15*, p. 321.

3 Klein, *Legacy of the Pharmacy Industry*, pp. 33-36.

4 Hugh S. Cooper, "Outline of Technical Activities of Hugh S. Cooper and Suggestions for Research Development and Manufacture," 1 September 1944, Hugh S. Cooper Papers, Kelvin Smith Library, Special Collections Research Center, Case Western Reserve University (hereafter: "Cooper Papers"), Box 1, folder 1; U.S. Patents 1,229,037 (1917), 1,248,621 (1917).

5 C. James, "Present State of the Production of Rarer Metals," *Transactions of the Electrochemical Society*, 43 (1923) 205, 214. Cooper delivered a paper on the preparation of fused zirconium immediately following James's presentation. The session on the production and application of the rarer metals was organized by Frederick Mark Becket.

6 *The Metal Industry* 15 (June 1917), 267. See for example Patent 1,461,173, filed in 1918 and assigned (by mense) to KEMET.

7 *Brass World and Plater's Guide* 17 (May 1921): 133; Cooper, "Outline of Technical Activities."

8 US Patent 1,254,987 (1918). See Kurt Illig, "The Production and Uses of Beryllium," *Transactions of the Electrochemical Society*, 54 (1928) 53-73.

9 Cooper claimed that he and Koelliker each received 25 percent of the stock, but the articles of incorporation suggest otherwise. Koelliker and Cooper would later sell their shares in KEMET Laboratories to Union Carbide. Cooper, "Outline of Technical Activities"; Corp 1661 KEMET Laboratories, Office of the County Clerk, Niagara Falls, New York.

10 Robert D. Stief, *A History of Union Carbide Corporation, from the 1890s to the 1990s* (Danbury: Carbide Retiree Corps, 1998), Ch. 1.

11 Jerry M. Fisher, *The Pacesetter: The Untold Story of Carl G. Fisher* (Northwestern University Press, 1998).

12 Raymond G. Stokes and Ralf Banken, *Building on Air: A History of the International Industrial Gases Industry, 1886-2006* (Cambridge University Press, 2016), 71.

13 Price would later go on to become a Vice President of Union Carbide. J. H. Brennan, H. E. Dunn, and C. M. Cosman, "Electric-furnace ferro-alloy industry in America," *Journal of Metals* 10 (1958) 786; Stief, *History of Union Carbide Corporation*, 12-16; Martha M. Trescott, *The Rise of the American Electrochemical Industry, 1880-1910: Studies in the American Technological Environment* (Greenwood Press, 1981); Edgar F. Price obituary, *Brooklyn Daily Eagle* 16 April 1935, p. 17.

14 Haynes, *American Chemical Industry*, II: 230; Trescott, *Rise of the American Electrochemical Industry*; Frederick M. Becket, "A Few Reflections on Forty Years of Research," *Transactions of the Electrochemical Society* 72 (1937) 14-24; "Frederick Mark Becket, 1875–1942: An Appreciation," *Mining and Metallurgy*, v. 24, no. 433 (Jan. 1943) 43; Frederick Mark Becket (Deceased) http://www.aimehq.org/about-us/presidents/frederick-mark-becket-deceased; Frederick Becket obituary, *Montreal Gazette*, 2 December 1942, p 13.

15 "United States Census, 1900," database with images, *FamilySearch*, Ohio > Summit > ED 75 Middlebury Township, Precinct D Akron city Ward 5 > image 17 of 46; citing NARA microfilmpublication T623 (Washington, D.C.: National Archives and Records Administration, n.d.).; "United States Census, 1910," database with images, *FamilySearch*, Ohio > Cuyahoga >Cleveland Ward 26 > ED 391 > image 8 of 10; citing NARA microfilm publication T624 (Washington, D.C.: National Archives and Records Administration, n.d.).

16 *Case Differential* 1912, p. 43; "Alumni News," *The Case Tech*, Volume XIV, Number 17, 28 February 1917, p. 3; "M. D. Sarbey Dies; Engineer and Wit," Cleveland Plain Dealer, 14 March 1940, p. 23.

17 US Patents 1,671,451 (1928); and 1,671,461 (1928); *Who's Who in Engineering*, 7th edition (1954), s.v. Bagley. For descriptions and use of the Sarbey furnace, see A. B. Kinzel, "Critical Points in Chromium-iron Alloys," *Iron and Steel Technology in 1928* (AIME 1928) 303; A. B. Kinzel and J. J. Egan, "Experimental Data on the Equilibrium of the System Iron Oxide-carbon in Molten Iron," *Transactions of the American Institute of Mining and Metallurgical Engineers Iron And Steel Division 1929* (AIME, 1929) 305-306.

18 Hugh S. Cooper, "Chronological Review of Research, Development and General Activities of Hugh S. Cooper. Period – 1914 to 1970," Cooper Papers, Box 1, folder 1; E. A. Engle and B. S. Hopkins, "The Metallurgy and Alloys of Beryllium," *Transactions of the American Electrochemical Society* 45 (1924), pp. 490-91; P. W. Bridgman, "The Compressibility and Pressure Coefficient of Resistence of Ten Elements," *Proceedings of the American Academy of Arts and Sciences*, 62 (1927) 214.

19 Hugh S. Cooper, *Beryllium: The Light Metal of the Future* (Beryllium Corporation of America, 1927), 14-16; US Patents 1,710,840 (1929) 1,775,589, and US1,805,567. Johann Boillat notes that the Berlin company of Siemens & Halske may have formed earlier. See his detailed discussion of Cooper and his contemporaries in "From Raw Material to Strategic Alloys: The Case of the International Beryllium Industry (1919-1939)," 10.13140/RG.2.2.35545.11363.

20 Cooper, "Chronological Review ... 1914 to 1970";
Hugh S. Cooper, "The Preparation of Fused Zirconium,
Transactions of the American Electrochemical Society
43 (1923), 215-230.

21 Williams Haynes, *Chemical Who's Who*, 3rd ed (1951),
p. 506; Menahem Merlub-Sobel, *Metals and Alloys
Dictionary* (Brooklyn: Chemical Publishing Company,
1944).

22 US Patent 1507987A (1924); US Patent 1,954,344
(1934); Thomas R. Cunningham, "A Method for
the Separation of Columbium and Tantalum"
(memorandum), Cooper Papers, Box 3, folder 8, and
US Patent 1908473A; Hugh S. Cooper to James A.
Holladay, 3 June 1932, Cooper Papers, Box 7, folder 26.
Memoranda from 1937 – after Cooper had parted ways
with Union Carbide – offered proposals for establishing
a plant that would produce 25 pounds of tantalum
per day, but he was unable to attract investors. Hugh
S. Cooper, "Tantalum Metal" (4-page proposal),
Cooper Papers, Box 7, folder 26; Maurice D. Sarbey to
J. S. Williams, 8 January 1937, Cooper Papers, Box 7,
folder 26.

CHAPTER TWO

1   H. J. B. Ward, Wireless Waves in the World's War, *The
Yearbook of Wireless Telegraphy and Telephony*, 1916,
pp. 625-644.

2   W. Rupert MacLaurin, *Invention and Innovation in the
Radio Industry* (New York: Macmillan, 1949), p 90.

3   Patent No. 1,244,217, issued 23 October 1917.

4   Arnold v. Langmuir, 36 F.2d 834, 17 CCPA 756 (1930).

5   Otto Schairer, *Patent Policies of Radio Corporation of
America* (New York: RCA institutes technical press,
1939), pp. 50, 62-63, 85.

6   John Dunning, *On the Air: The Encyclopedia of Old-
Time Radio* (New York: Oxford University Press, 1998),
pp. 235-236.

7   *Technology's War Record: An Interpretation of the
Contribution Made by the Massachusetts Institute of
Technology....* (Cambridge: MIT, 1920), p. 397.

8   The connections also spread across generations.
Huffard's son and grandson grew into leadership
positions at Union Carbide. Furness's daughter, Betty,
became an actress, a spokesperson for Westinghouse,
and the Special Assistant for Consumer Affairs under
President Lyndon B. Johnson.

9   Patent No. 1,730,326, filed 4 May 1925; Patent No.
1,730,723, filed 3 October 1925; Cooper, Chronological
Review of Research, Development, and General
Activities of Hugh S. Cooper. Period — 1914 to 1960,"
Cooper Papers, box folder p.3. The new design
worked better for electrical systems based on
alternating current (AC), which General Electric —
founced on Edison's devotion to direct current (DC)
had put off as long as possible.

10   Patent No. 1,661,235, filed 21 October 1925.

11   [Maurice D. Sarbey] to G[eorge] C. Furness, 26 May
1926, Cooper papers, box 7, folder 23.

12   Otto J. Scott, *The Creative Ordeal: The Story of
Raytheon* (New York: Athenaeum, 1974), pp. 35, 39,
48-49, 61, 66.

13   Patent No. 1,721,544, filed 14 April 1927; Patent No.
1,800,134, filed 31 December 1929.

14   Cooper, "Chronological Review ... to 1960," p. 4;
Patent No.1,908,473, filed 9 May 1931.

15   [Maurice D. Sarbey?], *Quarterly Report of KEMET
Laboratories Company, Inc., January 1st to April 1st,
1930*, Cooper Papers, Box 7, folder 23.

16   [Maurice D. Sarbey?], *Quarterly Report*, p. 2; Maurice
D. Sarbey memoranda to James A. Holladay, 1931-
1932, Cooper Papers, Box 5, folder 24.

17   Starting with patent no. 2,018,965, filed 10 November
1933.

18   Scott, *Creative Ordeal*, p. 13.

19   *Industrial Research Laboratories of the United States,
Including Consulting Research Laboratories*, 7th
edition (Washington, DC: National Research Council,
1940), pp. 279-282; https://www.electrochem.org/
critchett.

20   "James H. Critchett, Pres.: Officers Elected Yesterday
by Senior Class, M.I.T. – James I Finnie of Clinton Vice
President," *Boston Globe*, 27 Oct 1908 p. 8.

21   "Union Carbide II: Alloys, Gases, and Carbon,"
Fortune Magazine, July 1941, p. 92; *Industrial Research
Laboratories of the United States*, 5th edition (1933),
p. 107; *Industrial Research Laboratories of the United
States*, 8th edition (1946), p. 312; "Carbide and Carbon
Plant Rechristened by Parent Company," *Charleston
Gazette* 31 December 1949, p. 24.

22   U.S. Department of Commerce data aggregated in
Emil Onaca, *The Electronics Industry: Its Past-Present-
and Future* (Compton: Leach Corp.., 1962), p.3.

23   James Phinney Baxter III, *Scientists Against Time*
(Boston: Little, Brown, 1946), p. 142; War Production
Board, *Minutes of the War Production Board*, p. 304;
[J. A. Krug], *War Production: A Report to the War
Production Board* (GPO, 1944), p. 6.

24   Ray C. Ellis, "Wartime Radio Production,"
Proceedings of the I. R. E. (July 1943), p. 379.

25   "From Vaults to Guns," *War Production* (National
Association of Manufacturers), vol. 3 no. 7 (14
February 1942) p. 1; Ellis, "Wartime Radio Production,"
(July 1943), pp. 379-80; War Production Board,
*Minutes of the War Production Board: January 20,
1942, to October 9, 1944* (GPO, 1945), p. 304.

26   Department of Industrial Relations, Division of
Labor Statistics, *Directory of Manufactures in Ohio,
Labor Statistics Report No. 28* (1939), p. 112; idem,
Manufacturers' Directory, 1946, p. 60; Robert Hull,
Lakewood: Growing Up There (Bay Village, 1994),
p. 78.

27   Robert Slater, *Portraits in Silicon* (MIT Press, 1989),
p.78.

ENDNOTES

CHAPTER TWO, CONTINUED

28 Joseph H. Udelson, *The Great Television Race: A History of the American Television Industry, 1925-1941* (University of Alabama Press, 1982).

29 Alfred D. Chandler, Jr., *Inventing the Electronic Century: The Epic Story of the Consumer Electronics and Computer Industries* (Harvard University Press, 2005), p. 28.

30 Ohio Department of Industrial Relations, Division of Labor Statistics, *Manufacturers' Directory, 1951*, p. 230; idem, *Manufacturers' Directory, 1954*, p. 24; idem, *Manufacturers' Directory, 1956*, p. 323.

CHAPTER THREE

1 Christophe Lécuyer and David C. Brock, *Makers of the Microchip: A Documentary History of Fairchild Semiconductor* (Cambridge: MIT Press, 2010), p. 11.

2 Ironically, the new Union Carbide Electronics division was established by Jean Hoerni, who had worked at Shockley Semiconductor and Amelco Semiconductor. He left Union Carbide after only three years, saying, "Semiconductors are not Union Carbide's cup of tea," and went on to invent the integrated circuit. John E. Tilton, *International Diffusion of Technology: The Case of Semiconductors* (Brookings Institution Press, 1971), pp. 51-52; Bo Lojek, *History of Semiconductor Engineering* (Springer Verlag, 2007), p. 223.

3 "Dedicate New Carbon Co. Research Lab," *Bennington Evening Banner*, 18 September 1956, p. 8; James F. Mauk, ed., *Industrial Research Laboratories of the United States*, 10th ed. (National Academy of Sciences, 1956), 3724.

4 R. L. Taylor and H. E. Haring, "A Metal Semi-Conductor Capacitor," *Journal of the Electrochemical Society* 103 (1956) 611-13.

5 Patent No. 3,066,247, filed 25 August 1954, approved 27 November 1962.

6 Patent No. 2,936,514 (Millard), filed 24 October 1955, approved 17 May 1960.

7 "Sprague Wins: Bell Laboratories Drop Suit to Wrest Patent from Concern," *North Adams Transcript*, 8 April 1964, p. 5.

8 *Union Carbide Annual Report 1957*, p. 25; *Union Carbide Annual Report 1958*, p. 21.

9 "Union Carbide Gets License to Use Sprague Electric Patents," *Bennington Banner*, 7 August 1964, p. 5.

10 Siegfried Wagener, *Die Berechnung der Gittertemperatur von Empfängerröhren* (Berlin, 1935); Siegfried Wagener and Günther Herrmann, *The Oxide-Coated Cathode*, 2 vols. (London: Chapman & Hall, 1951); Siegfried Wagener, "The Cosmic Cocktail," *Wonder Stories*, April 1936; Renate Tobies, *Iris Runge: A Life at the Crossroads of Mathematics, Science, and Industry* (Basel: Birkhäuser, 2012), pp. 284, 346; *Who's Who in Science in Europe* (1967) p. 1644.

11 Howard Pattin obituary, *Cleveland Plain Dealer*, 1 5 August 1988, p. 18.

12 Bureau of Mines, *Minerals Yearbook 1962*, I: 469.

13 Union Carbide, *Our History* (Union Carbide Public Relations Department, 1974), pp. 3-7.

14 Wayne Hazen interview, 11 April 2019.

15 Union Carbide, *Annual Report for 1961*, p. 30.

16 "Carbide Plans to Expand Activities in Electronics," *Paducah Sun* (Paducah, Kentucky), 29 June 1962, p. 22.

17 Wayne Hazen interview.

18 Although scientists generally see meeting new specifications as an engaging challenge, poorly conceived standards raise their ire. Two KEMET managers wrote an angry article to protest a new government specification for military contracts that had contradictory directives. John Makhijani and Richard H. Robecki, "The Sizzle and the Steak," *Concept* 3:6 (January 1969).

19 Dale Hazen interview, 12 April 2019.

20 "Maguire Moves from Carbide to Kemet Unit," *Fremont News-Messenger*, 8 February 1961, p. 3.

21 U.S. Patent 3,458,803, filed 21 March 1966, assigned 29 July 1969.

22 David E. Maguire, "Improved Tantalum Chip Capacitors for Hybrid Circuits," *Proceedings of the 1969 Electrical Components Conference* (Washington, DC), pp. 211-217.

23 "Union Carbide to Build Plant on 40-Acre Simpsonville Site," *Greenville News*, 7 February 1963, p. 48.

24 Greenville Plant Components Department, memorandum, January 1974, KEMET archives, Simpsonville, SC, p. 3.

25 Bonnie Craven interview, 11 April 2019.

26 Jeanette Simpson interview, 11 April 2019.

27 Dick Thompson interview, 12 April 2019.

28 Tom Roper, "Straight Talk: '73 Broke All Records," *KEMET Topics*, 1: 1 (January, 1974), p. 1.

29 Bill Hazen interview, 11 April 2019.

30 Dale Hazen interview, 12 April 2019.

31 Erwin Fischler, interview, 20 June 2019; Brian Hawthornthwaite interview, 5 April 2019.

32 "Seventh Year — KEMET Receives Vendor Excellence Award from Raytheon Company," *KEMET Topics*, 8:1 (January 1980), p. 4.

33 Warren M. Anderson, "An Important Message to Employees," *Union Carbide World*, January/February 1986.

CHAPTER FOUR

1 Dona d J. Poinsette interview, 29 May 2019.

2 Heller Financial, Inc., Capital Markets Group, *Confidential Direct Placement Memorandum: KEMET Electronics Corporation*, February 1991, Exhibit E.

3 *KEMET Annual Report* 1995, p. 5.

4 Yuri Freeman, *Tantalum and Niobium-Based Capacitors: Science, Technology, and Applications*, p. xvii.

5 "KEMET, NEC Extend Ta Cap Pact," *Electronic News* 21 June 1999.

6 John Piper, "Tantalum chip capacitors pack high value into hybrid circuits," *Electronics*, 18 January 1971, p. 68.

7 *Executive Viewpoint*, KEMET Electronics, 1989, p. 3.

8 Norm Alster, "Moving Up In A Commodity Chip Business," *Investor's Business Daily*, Oct. 25, 1995.

9 "KEMET Electronics Buy-Out," *The Wall Street Journal*, Dec. 26, 1990.

10 Lee Ann Fleet, "KEMET to begin public trading," *Greenville News*, Oct. 21, 1992.

11 *KEMET Annual Reports 1993-1996.*

12 William Langewiesche. "The Border," *Atlantic Monthly* 269 (June 1992), pp. 91-108; Maria Guadalupe Torres Martinez, "Violations of Women's Human Rights in Maquiladoras," in Niamh Reilly, ed., *Without Reservation: The Beijing Tribunal on Accountability for Women's Human Rights* (New Brunswick, NJ: Center for Women's Global Leadership, 1996), pp. 82-86.

13 "KEMET providing parts for repairs on Mir station," *Greenville News,* 13 July 1997, p. 17.

14 Anne P. Thrower, "KEMET Corp. president resign; company has new structure," *Greenfield News,* 4 November 1997, p. 34.

15 *KEMET Annual Report 1997*, p. 10.

16 Bernard Levine, "KEMET to Vishay: No Way," *Electronic News*, 8 July 1996, p. 90.

17 Bernard Levine "Vishay Still Woos Kemet," *Electronic News,* 5 August 1996, p. 6.

18 *Henderson's Electronic Market Forecast*, September 1990.

19 Judy _ynn, "KEMET Corp. on the Rebound," *The Greenville Journal*, Sept. 10-16, 1999

20 Chad Bray, "KEMET names new president, COO," *Greenville News*, 24 June 1999, p. 27.

21 *KEMET Annual Report 2002*, p. 6.

22 Jenny Munro, "KEMET names new CEO," *Greenfield News,* 26 March 2003, p. 9

23 "Street Talk," *Greenville News*, 19 December 2004, p. 9.

24 Kirk Cheyfitz, *Thinking inside the Box: The 12 Timeless Rules for Managing a Successful Business* (Simon & Schuster, 2003), pp. 30-32.

25 *KEMET Annual Report 2004*, p. 6.

26 Woody White, "KEMET restructuring, cutting jobs," *Greenville News,* 28 June 2005, p. 9; *KEMET Annual Report 2005*, p. 2.

27 *KEMET Annual Report 2007*, p. 2.

28 *KEMET Annual Report 2006*, p. 3.

29 Richard F. Stevens, Jr., "Columbium and Tantalum," in Bureau of Mines, *Minerals Yearbook: Metals and Minerals (except fuels)*, 1964 (Washington, D.C.: Government Printing Office, 1965), vol. 1, p. 401.

30 KEMET, Program in Conflict-Free DRC Mining Community, Aug 25, 2015. https://www.prnewswire.com/news-releases/kemet-leads-humanitarian-program-in-conflict-free-drc-mining-community-300132975.html.

31 *KEMET Annual Report 2009*, pp. 1-2.

32 Ross Kerber, "Lights, Camera, CEO?," *Boston Globe*, 28 May 2007, p. D1.

CHAPTER FIVE

1 Philip Lessner, interview.

2 KEMET Annual Report 2018, p. 9.

3 Patent US3299325A, filed 29 January 1963; Patent US3337429A, filed 28 May 1964.

4 Patent US3553805A, filed 22 April 1969.

5 Patent US3611054A, filed 2 March 1970.

6 Philip Lessner, interview.

7 For example, patent US7563290, filed 6 July 2006.

8 Chuck Meeks interview, 16 August 2018.

9 Patent US7172985, filed 7 June 2005.

10 *KEMET Annual Report* 2010, p. [iii].

11 Scott Miller, "Clemson Expands high-powered microscopy lab for research and industry use," *The Newsstand*, 29 January 2019. https://newsstand.clemson.edu/mediarelations/clemsonexpands-high-powered-microscopy-lab-for-research-and-industry-use/

12 Jess Almodovar, "What is KAIC?," 4 March 2019. https://ec.kemet.com/what-is-kaic

IMAGE CREDITS

Front cover, left to right:

Row 1 4503 Euclid Avenue: Cleveland Public Library/ Photograph Collection.
Hugh S. Cooper: Courtesy of Hugh and Beverly Cooper.
Union Carbide personnel: courtesy of the Niagara Falls Public Library.
National Carbon building: Cleveland Memory Project, Michael Schwartz Library, Cleveland State University.
Vacuum tube: KEMET Archives.

Row 2 KEMET Archives.

Row 3 Autonomous car: iStock.com/metamorworks.
James Webb Space Telescope: NASA/MSFC/David Higginbotham.
Futuristic auto touch screen: iStock.com/ metamorworks.
Electronics technology: iStock.com/ metamorworks.
Broadcast satellite: iStock.com/beaucroft.

Row 4 Robotic auto production: iStock.com/xieyuliang.
Smart city: iStock.com/jamesteohart.
Wind turbines/Solar panels: iStock.com/ imacoconut.
Autonomous car: iStock.com/metamorworks.
Smart traffic system concept: iStock.com/Wenjie Dong.

4 Portrait of Hugh Cooper: Courtesy of Hugh and Beverly Cooper.

5 Vacuum tube. From Paul V. Malloy, Patent 2,126,686, filed 11 February 1936; Cooper Patent: Patent 1,229,037. Filed 14 August 1915; KEMET workers: KEMET, *Getters and Gettering Methods for Electron Tubes* (Cleveland: Kemet Company, ca. 1948), p.7, From the Hugh S. Cooper Papers, Kelvin Smith Library Special Collections, Case Western Reserve University (hereafter cited as "Cooper Papers"), Box 3, Folder 9.

6 Margaret A. Hittle, *Steel Mill*, mural, Lane Tech High School, Chicago. Courtesy of The Conservation Center in Chicago and Heather Becker, author of *Art for the People*.

7 Prospect Avenue and E. 40th Street, Cleveland: City of Cleveland Board of Zoning Appeals case files (Calendar No. 46-684).

8 *Scientific American*, 2 April 1881.

9 Charles F. Brush. Charles F. Brush, Sr. papers, Kelvin Smith Library Special Collections, Case Western Reserve University, series 13: photographs.

10 Hugh S. Cooper, Patent 1,229,037. Filed 14 August 1915.

11 Cuyahoga Building: Cleveland Memory Project, Michael Schwartz Library, Cleveland State University.

12 KEMET stationary: Courtesy of Hugh and Beverly Cooper.

13 4503 Euclid Avenue: Cleveland Public Library / Photograph Collection.

14 Article on Cooperite: *Brass World and Platers' Guide*, vol. XVII, no. 5 (May 1921), p. 133.

15 KEMET annual meeting: Corp File 1661, County Clerk's Office, Niagara County, New York.

17 William J. Knapp: Courtesy of George Owen Knapp III.

17 Union Carbide and Carbon Building: Museum of the City of New York.

19 Frederick Mark Becket: Courtesy of ECS – The Electrochemical Society.

20 Maurice Sarbey: Courtesy of Marty Souto-Martinez.

21 Sarbey Furnace: illustration from A. B. Kinsel, "Critical Points in Chromium-iron Alloys," *Iron and Steel Technology in 1928* (American Institute Of Mining And Metallurgical Engineers, 1928), p. 302.

23 Harold F. Blanchard, "Beryllium — The Wonder Metal," *MoToR: The Automotive Business Paper*, May 1928, pp. 30-31; Patent memorandum: Cooper Papers Box 16, Folder 1.

24 Sarbey furnace: Cooper Papers Box 16, Folder 1; KEMET chemistry lab: Courtesy of Hugh and Beverly Cooper.

25 KEMET lab equipment: all courtesy of Hugh and Beverly Cooper. The author gratefully acknowledges the guidance of Antoine Allanore, Professor of Metallurgy at the Massachusetts Institute of Technology, in identifying these apparatus.

26 Furnace: Cooper Papers Box 16, Folder 1; power plant: Courtesy of Hugh and Beverly Cooper.

27 Menahem Merlub-Sobel: Nessyahu Historical Archive, Elyachar Central Library, Technion: Israel Institute of Technology. Blueprint for ammonia cracking apparatus: Cooper Papers, Box 7, Folder 22.

28 Electro-Metallurgical Company personnel: Courtesy of the Niagara Falls Public Library.

29 George C. Furness: Courtesy of Babbie Green.

31 Edison light bulbs: Library of Congress, Prints & Photographs Division, PAGA 7, no. 281 (E size); Barium: Copyright © 2019 Theodore Gray, periodictable.com; Irving Langmuir and colleagues: Library of Congress, Prints & Photographs Division, LC-B2- 6197-6; Iconoscope: Vladimir Zworykin and television tube: Courtesy of the Hagley Museum and Library: Early television: *Radio & Appliance Journal*, August 1947, p.27.

IMAGE CREDITS

83 Production processes: KEMET Archives.

84 Advertisement: KEMET Archives.

85 Production leadership: *KEMET Topics*, vol. 1 no. 1 (January 1974), p. 2.

86 ISO 9000 meeting: KEMET Archives

87 KEMET personnel and Westinghouse award: KEMET Archives.

88 Floor plans: *Welcome to our 10th Anniversary Salute ... to you* (Greenville, SC: Union Carbide Components Department, 1973), verso.

90 Contract signing: KEMET Archives.

91 KEMET Suzhou, Per-Olof Loof, Kisengo miners: All KEMET Archives.

92-93 Fab 14: All KEMET Archives except James Jerozal (courtesy of James Jerozal) and Ed Bost (courtesy of Wanda Bazemore).

94 KEMET/Avnet ad: KEMET Archives.

95 Flying capacitors: KEMET Archives. Ford TQE Award: Inside KEMET, vol. 9, n.4 (July/August 1994), p. 1.

96 Capacitor cross-sections: KEMET Archives.

100 KEMET de México: All KEMET Archives.

101 KEMET de México: All KEMET Archives.

102 Board of Directors: *KEMET Annual Report* 1993, p. 36.

103 Maria Guadalupe Torres: *The Monitor* (McAllen, Texas), 17 March 1991, p.19.

104 *KEMET Annual Report* 1993.

106 Microprocessor applications: All KEMET Archives.

107 Automotive applications: top and bottom KEMET Archives; middle: iStock.com/metamorworks; iStock.com/xieyuliang.

108 Medicine: All KEMET Archives except Glucose Meter: iStock.com/AlexRaths.

109 Aerospace: All KEMET Archives.

111 *Electronic News*, vol. 42, No. 2124 (8 July 1996), p.1.

112 Cross-section: KEMET Archives.

113 Charles M. Culbertson II: KEMET Archives.

114 The first billion: KEMET Archives.

115 KEMET personnel: KEMET Archives.

116 Nasdaq Chart: Bloomberg.

120 KEMET personnel: All KEMET Archives.

121 KEMET personnel: All KEMET Archives.

122 Kisengo Foundation: KEMET Archives.

123 Kisengo Foundation: KEMET Archives.

127 Tokin personnel: KEMET Archives.

128 KEMET scientist: KEMET Archives.

129 John Piper and Gordon Love: KEMET Archives.

130 Tantalum team: KEMET Archives.

131 KEMET Suzhou: KEMET Archives.

132 KEMET scientists: KEMET Archives.

133 KEMET Japan: KEMET Archives.

134 KEMET products: KEMET Archives.

135 KEMET products: KEMET Archives.

136 KEMET personnel: KEMET Archives.

137 KEMET personnel: KEMET Archives.

138 KEMET KONNEKT: KEMET Archives.

139 KEMET personnel: KEMET Archives.

141 KIAIC: KEMET Archives.

142 Roadway: Asoggetti on Unsplash.

143 Smart Home: iStock.com/bagotaj. Interconnected city: iStock.com/ansonmiao.

144 Piezoelectric plate: KEMET Archives.

145 Astronaut: NASA on Unsplash.

146 Wind turbine: iStock.com/Harry Wedzinga.

147 High school intern: KEMET Archives.

Back cover, left to right:
Row 1 Preston Robinson: *Sprague Electric Log*, v. 14 n. 18](2 May 1952), p.1.
Getter test: KEMET, *Getters and Gettering Methods for Electron Tubes*, p. 5.
Ceramic capacitor machinery and cutting: KEMET Archives.
George C. Furness: Courtesy of Babbie Green.

Row 2 KEMET Archives.

Row 3 KEMET Archives.

Row 4 Artifical Intelligence: iStock.com/kynny.
Semiconductor: iStock.com/CasarsaGuru.
Server computers: iStock.com/undefined.